A GIFT

To: Marlene

From: Secret Prayer Partner

Date: 2000

FOR YOU

COUNT
YOUR
BLESSINGS

A Daily Devotional of Praise and Thanksgiving

Compiled by Catherine L. Davis

ChariotVICTOR
PUBLISHING
A DIVISION OF COOK COMMUNICATIONS

Unless otherwise noted, all Scripture references are from
the *Holy Bible, New International Version*®. Copyright© 1973,
1978, 1984 by International Bible Society. Used by permission
of Zondervan Publishing House. All rights reserved; other
references are from the *Authorized (King James) Version* (KJV);
The Living Bible (TLB),© 1971, Tyndale House Publishers,
Wheaton, IL 60189. Used by permission; the *New American
Standard Bible* (NASB), © the Lockman Foundation 1960, 1962,
1963, 1968, 1971, 1972, 1973, 1975, 1977; *The New King
James Version* (NKJV). © 1979, 1980, 1982, Thomas Nelson,
Inc., Publishers.

Copyright © 1997 by Victor Books

ISBN 1-56476-693-4

Editor: Barb Williams

Art Director: Bill Gray

Designer: Big Cat Studios, Inc.

Original Cover Artwork: © Kathy Jakobsen, Licensed by Wild Apple
Licensing.

Printed in Canada.
1 2 3 4 5 6 7 8 9 10 Printing/Year 01 00 99 98 97

Victor Books is an imprint of ChariotVictor Publishing,
a division of Cook Communications, Colorado Springs,
Colorado 80918
Cook Communications, Paris, Ontario
Kingsway Communications, Eastbourne, England

He satisfies my desires with good things,
so that my youth is renewed like the eagle's.

(P S A L M *1 0 3 : 5*)

FOREWORD

There are many lessons in life that teach us to be thankful, that remind us to close our eyes and take a moment to be silent and grateful.

One experience that I am drawn back to is the sight of an old house on a dirt road back in the hills of Tennessee, just down the road from where we lived. Whenever we stopped by, it always seemed so sad—laundry hanging out on the porch, a yard cluttered with trash and the remains of old cars. Inside the house, chickens roamed freely.

But that wasn't the saddest part. Every time we were there, the mother yelled at her children and told them how worthless they were—while the father remained silent.

One Christmas my family decided to take a fruit basket to these neighbors, along with a present for each of the boys. As we handed them the gifts, looks I will never forget appeared on their faces: shock that someone had thought of them; humility; but, most of all, gratefulness. Though life had handed them a difficult path, they were not jaded from the joy of that moment.

That event forced me to think of all the simple gifts most of us are blessed with regularly, from a meal to the warmth of a sunny day. We must find the place inside which asks for no more and find pleasure in what we have already been given.

It seems in learning more of the wonder and the mystery of life, the greatest miracle of all comes not in receiving gifts but in knowing the Giver of all gifts.

I pray that the words of this book will inspire us to seek the treasure of knowing God in our hearts and to count all of our blessings this side of heaven.

CINDY MORGAN
Christian Recording Artist

COUNT YOUR BLESSINGS

I will extol the Lord at all times;
his praise will always be on my lips.

(PSALM 34:1)

Would you know who is the greatest saint in the
world? It is not he who prays most or fasts most. It is
not he who gives the most money . . . but it is he who
is always thankful to God, who wills everything that
God wills, and who receives everything as an instance
of God's goodness and has a heart always ready to
praise God for it.

William Law

Thou hast given so much to me,
Give me one more thing—a grateful heart,
Not thankful when it pleases me,
As if Thy blessings had spare days,
But such a heart
Whose pulse may be Thy praise.

George Herbert

Praise the Lord. Give thanks to the Lord,
for he is good; his love endures forever.

(PSALM *106:1*)

The Christian with the spirit of gratitude finds his prayers become *prayers of praise, adoration, and thanksgiving to God.* "Lord, thank You." He rests on the utter dependability of God to accomplish everything He promises, whether a blessing or a threat against sin. It is the most sublime state: a full, total, complete, unequivocal, no retreat, no regrets surrender to Christ. Gladness of heart occupies his thoughts, regardless of circumstantial strains. Beams of gratitude continually shine warmth on the personal relationship with Christ.

The grateful saint still prays for needs and still seeks the will of God, but a spirit of gratitude overarches every utterance to God. Praise and adoration accompany every visit to the throne of grace.

Patrick M. Morley

Lord, I want my life to be a continual praise to Your name. You are my joy, my hope, my life.

Jesus spoke all these things to the crowd in parables;
he did not say anything to them without using a parable.
So was fulfilled what was spoken through the prophet:
"I will open my mouth in parables, I will utter things
hidden since the creation of the world."

(MATTHEW 13:34-35)

It was said of Jesus that the common people heard him gladly; and no wonder, for the extraordinary quality of his teachings, and especially of his parables, was that they said what ordinary men and women could take hold of. When Jesus spoke, it was not as though some unfamiliar idea were coming from outside, but rather as though an instinctive recognition were being awakened in the listeners' own selves. "That is the way life really works," they felt. "That is how truth is." The parables did not bring alien information; rather they focused and called into action what people already half knew was so, and now suddenly could fully see.

The Interpreter's Bible, Vol. 7

Thank You, Jesus, for the word pictures You gave us
to help understand Your truth.

Nothing in all creation is hidden from God's sight.
Everything is uncovered and laid bare before the eyes
of him to whom we must give account.

(HEBREWS 4:13)

I'm so glad God can read my heart and understand what's going on even when I am handicapped by my own weakness for words. As it says in this verse, "Nothing . . . is hidden from God's sight."

Words are not always necessary. When we are in such trouble that we can't even find words—when we can only look toward Heaven and groan in our spirit— isn't it good to remember that God knows exactly what's happening? The faintest whisper in our hearts is known to God. Even if it should be a sigh so faint that you are not even aware of it yourself, He has heard it. And not only heard it, but He *understands* it—right down to the slightest quiver registered in our inner- most being. . . . The Spirit is never handicapped by our weakness for words.

Joni Eareckson Tada

You know the unspoken words of my heart.
Thank You that You know . . . and understand.

When the centurion and those with him who were guarding Jesus saw the earthquake and all that happened, they were terrified, and exclaimed, "Surely he was the Son of God!"

(MATTHEW 27:54)

Lew Wallace, author of *Ben Hur*, was challenged by the noted agnostic, Robert G. Ingersoll, to give the world a book that would prove the falsity of Jesus Christ. Wallace spent many years traveling abroad researching ancient manuscripts. But, as he started to write, he realized that all his research had only proved that Jesus Christ was real in history. He became more convinced that Christ not only lived but He was divine, resurrected, and was the Saviour of men. At 50 years of age he prayed for the first time and accepted Christ as his Saviour. He rewrote his manuscript and gave the world *Ben Hur* to prove that Christ is the son of God and the Saviour of the world.

Henry Gariepy

Jesus Christ, Son of God, I praise You for coming to live and die as a man, for giving us a glimpse of God, for paying the price for the sins of the world.

*The man who enters by the gate is the
shepherd of his sheep. The watchman opens
the gate for him, and the sheep listen to his
voice. He calls his own sheep by name
and leads them out.*

(J O H N *10 : 2 - 3*)

There have been moments in all of our lives when
we've experienced God's voice. We may not have
understood it, but we sensed Him speaking, sensed it
was our name He was calling. Some of those moments
may have been in dreams. In some of those dreams, He
tells us a story maybe, or maybe rubs away the growing
pains in our soul. Or He may tell us how proud He is to
be our Father. A kid needs to hear that. A lot. He tells
us that often throughout the day, but sometimes
bedtime is the best time to hear it, when all the toys
are put up and the books are back on the shelves and
the spirit is still.

Ken Gire

*Thank You for the times when I have sensed
Your voice . . . and for the reassurance that You
are <u>always</u> my caring Heavenly Father.*

Do not be afraid of what you are about to suffer. . . .
Be faithful, even to the point of death, and I will
give you the crown of life.

(REVELATION 2:10)

For those who have suffered incurable illnesses, terrible heartache, or who have suffered their whole life long for their faith, it would be almost unkind to say, "Well, it won't be long before you are in heaven." But actually, this Scripture has done that, not as a way of dismissing pain but as a way of recognizing it and the brevity of life, as well as the joy of eternal life in Christ and the crown that awaits us.

"Be faithful, even to the point of death." Hold steady until you die. That is what our Lord is saying. And actually that is not a very long time to hold steady, not when we consider all of eternity. This is an encouraging word, not a word of casual dismissal of our pain. Hold on until death. Hold on until your coronation. The promise is there, "I will give you the crown of life." The Word of God puts into perspective the pain experienced by so many of God's people.

Roger Palms

Thank You, Lord, that no matter what happens, You promise
strength to hold on until "crowning day."

And beginning with Moses and all the Prophets,
he explained to them what was said in all the
Scriptures concerning himself.

(LUKE 24:27)

The B–I–B–L–E,
Yes, that's the book for me.
I stand alone on the Word of God.
The B–I–B–L–E!

O God, we thank you for all those in whose words and
in whose writings your truth has come to us.
For the historians, the psalmists and the prophets,
who wrote the Old Testament;
For those who wrote the Gospels and the Letters
of the New Testament;
For all who in every generation have taught and explained and
expounded and preached the word of Scripture:
We thank you, O God.

William Barclay

*Each one should use whatever gift he has received
to serve others, faithfully administering
God's grace in its various forms.*

(1 PETER 4:10)

Somewhere I heard a story about Michelangelo's pushing a huge rock down a street. A curious neighbor sitting lazily on the porch of his house called to him and inquired why he labored so over an old piece of stone. Michelangelo is reported to have answered, "Because there is an angel in that rock that wants to come out."

This story comes to mind when I think about the gifts or talents given to each of us. Every person has the task of releasing angels by shaping and transfiguring the raw materials that lie about him so that they become houses and machinery and pictures and bridges. How we do this—how we "build the earth," to use Teilhard de Chardin's phrase—is determined by the discovery and the use of our gifts.

Elizabeth O'Connor

*"Each one" means me too, Lord. How good You are to
give each of us a way to praise You with our lives.*

You show that you are a letter from Christ, the result of our ministry, written not with ink but with the Spirit of the living God, not on tablets of stone but on tablets of human hearts.

(2 CORINTHIANS 3:3)

It is good to experience the quiet ministry of the living spirit of the living God. Again and again there are the little healings of silent breaches which sustain us in our contacts with the world and with one another. . . . There are problems that meet us head-on in our journey. . . . It seems that nowhere, in no place, can an answer be found. . . . Again and again it is apt to happen: the miracle of relief; a chance word from a casual conversation; a sentiment or a line in a letter; the refrain of an old song; an image from the past; a paragraph from a printed page . . . the danger is passed, the conflict is over. It is good, so very good, to experience the quiet ministry of the living spirit of the living God.

Howard Thurman

Spirit of the Living God, I'm grateful for Your quiet ministry in my heart and in the hearts of those I'll meet today.

*In my Father's house are many rooms; if it were not so,
I would have told you. I am going there to prepare
a place for you.*

(J O H N *14 : 2*)

What will heaven be like,
whether I go there as a result of this
operation (a remote possibility),
or go there later (a certainty)?
Heaven will be my eternal
home with Christ. I'll just move
into the part of his Father's
house he prepared for me. No fixing
up that home, no parts unfinished,
no disappointments on moving day.
No, he's prepared it, he's made it
completely ready, completely
perfect, completely mine.

Joseph Bayly

*Thank You, Father, for the home that awaits me …
forever … with You.*

He satisfies my desires with good things,
so that my youth is renewed like the eagle's.

(PSALM 103:5)

I made a hospital call on a parishioner just before her death last year, and we were able to talk about her situation. She said, "It's a little untimely. I would like to have lived a little longer, but I am facing it." We prayed together, and I was about to leave when she made an unusual request. "Would you come over here and feel my hair?" I did so. "You know, before chemotherapy my hair was white. It's now come in black. All my life I've had straight hair, and wished it was otherwise. This new growth of hair is curly. Isn't the Lord good? I'm going to die with black, curly hair." I left that room deeply moved. My friend would die, but she was dying unafraid and full of thanksgiving to God.

Bruce Larson

Thank You for those unexpected expressions of Your love.

Our Father which art in heaven, Hallowed be thy name ...
Give us this day our daily bread.

(MATTHEW 6:9B,11, KJV)

Just as God provides the physical necessities and satis-
factions of all creatures—the bird and the fox and the
ear of corn and the flower—so He also has provided for
human economic needs, The physical and the material
are as "religious" as any other facet of living. Abundant
living is a right relationship with all life, and it is
evidence of a free expectancy and a bold claiming of
what is rightfully ours by the will of the Creator.

When we say, "Give us this day our daily bread," we
should say it with the arms of expectancy stretched out
to receive, and with our hearts bursting with gratitude,
adoration, and love for the beneficence of God. In
seeking first the Kingdom of God we cultivate and
tune ourselves to the abundancies of heaven, and make
friends with them. . . . *Give us this day our daily bread*
means the discovery of God operating, guiding, and
providing in our entire economic structure. He is
always there, waiting to "burst out like a flood" . . . if
we will but provide Him a channel of manifestation by
our asking, expectancy, claiming, and serving.

Norman Elliott

You are faithful, God, to provide for my physical needs, and more.

I sought the Lord, and he answered me;
he delivered me from all my fears.

(PSALM 34:4)

What my end will be and what I shall become, I do not know. But I am to the point that a peace of soul and rest of spirit descend upon me even when I am asleep. To be without this sense, this constant sense of peace, would be suffering indeed; but with peace in my inner being I believe I could find consolation even in purgatory.

No, I do not know what God purposes with me, nor what is in store for me. But I am in a calm so great that I fear nothing. What could I fear? I am with Him. And there, with Him, in His presence, is where I keep myself all I can.

May all things praise Him.

Brother Lawrence

Sometimes my fears block the sense of Your presence, but You are there, tenderly calling me to a new trust and calm.

But thanks be to God, who always leads us in triumphal procession in Christ and through us spreads everywhere the fragrance of the knowledge of him. For we are to God the aroma of Christ among those who are being saved and those who are perishing.

(2 C O R I N T H I A N S 2 : 1 4 - 1 5)

Doing something beautiful for God is, for Mother Teresa, what life is about. Everything, in that it is for God, becomes beautiful, whatever it may be; as does every human soul participating in this purpose, whoever he or she may be. In manifesting this, in themselves and in their lives and work, Mother Teresa and the Missionaries of Charity provide a living witness to the power and truth of what Jesus came to proclaim. His light shines in them. When I think of them in Calcutta, as I often do, it is not the bare house in a dark slum that is conjured up in my mind, but a light shining and a joy abounding. I see them diligently and cheerfully constructing something beautiful for God out of the human misery and affliction that lies around them. One of their leper settlements is near a slaughter-house whose stench in the ordinary way might easily make me retch. There, with Mother Teresa, I scarcely noticed it; another fragrance had swallowed it up.

Malcolm Muggeridge

What a privilege, God, to be the fragrance of Christ to my world.

*In Joppa there was a disciple named Tabitha
(which when translated, is Dorcas), who was always
doing good and helping the poor.*

(ACTS 9:36)

LaVon 's entire life was devoted to meeting the needs
of her large family (six children and fourteen grand-
children) and her many friends. Even as she lay dying
of cancer in severe pain she found ways to look out for
the interests of those she loved: she provided engraved
Bibles for her children to be delivered on their birth-
days; she gave each grandchild a framed picture of
Jesus with a handwritten, personal note on the back,
she spent quality time with each family member to say
a special good-bye and make sure they were right with
the Lord; she exhorted others with cards and phone
calls until she could no longer write or talk; and she
made sure that, when she was no longer able, her
personal funds continued to be distributed all over the
country for the furtherance of the Gospel and the
support of God's workers. LaVon was able to maintain
her joy, even to the tragic end of her earthly life,
because of her partnership with Christ and her partnership with others.

Roger Palms

*Bless You, God, and bless those who have blessed me
because they are in partnership with You.*

"Abba, Father," he said, "everything is possible for you. Take this cup from me. Yet not what I will, but what you will."

(MARK 14:36)

What difference did Jesus make? Both for God and for us, he made possible an *intimacy* that had never before existed. In the Old Testament, Israelites who touched the sacred Ark of the Covenant fell down dead; but people who touched Jesus, the Son of God in flesh, came away healed. To Jews who would not pronounce or even spell out the letters in God's name, Jesus taught a new way of addressing God: *Abba*, or "Daddy." In Jesus, God came close.

Philip Yancey

Jesus, I praise You for making it possible for me to call God my "Abba."

For to me, to live is Christ and to die is gain.

(PHILIPPIANS 1:21)

Only of this I am assured, that some time and in some way, spirit to spirit, face to face, I shall meet the great Lord of life, and, falling before Him tell my gratitude for all He has done, and implore pardon for all I have left undone.

Paul Elmer More

Life is worthwhile, dear God,
To those who know
This rich companionship with Thee;
Each morning as the day flames forth,
Each evening in a sweet tranquillity.

Ten million million gifts
Spring from Thy hand,
Of up-flung mountains, evening skies, a tree!
Yet never one can quite compare with this—
The giving of Thyself to me!

Ralph S. Cushman

Now when he saw the crowds, he went up on a mountainside
and sat down. His disciples came to him, and he began to
teach them, saying: "Blessed are ..."

(M A T T H E W   5 : 1 - 3 A)

The Beatitudes are Jesus' self-portrait, the most
personal description we have of Him in the Gospels.
They are the timeless image of Christ.

. . . We have often longed to know what Jesus actually looked like. What would a painting, a photograph
have shown us? Would we today recognize Him if we
saw Him? Although the mystery of the face of Jesus
remains, each of us carries his own inner picture of
Him. Consciously or unconsciously we are always looking for the Christ figure Who walks into each of our
lives; each of hopes for a secret or unexpected
rendezvous. . . Yet it is in the Beatitudes that we truly
recognize Him.

Edward Farrell

There You are, Jesus, there on the mountain,
showing us who You really are through what You taught.
Thank You for that intimate, timeless image.

May the God of hope fill you with all joy and peace
as you trust in him, so that you may overflow with hope
by the power of the Holy Spirit.

(ROMANS 15:13)

As we go forth into the coming year, let it not be in the haste of impetuous, unremembering delight, nor with the flight of impulsive thoughtlessness, but with the patient power of knowing that the God of Israel will go before us. Our yesterdays present irreparable things to us; it is true that we have lost opportunities which will never return, but God can tranform this destructive anxiety into a constructive thoughtfulness for the future. Let the past sleep, but let it sleep on the bosom of Christ.

Leave the Irreparable Past in His hands, and step out into the Irresistible Future with Him.

Oswald Chambers

I praise You, God of hope, that my past can sleep
on the bosom of Christ, and that I can step out
into the future without anxiety.

Make every effort to keep the unity of the Spirit through the
bond of peace. There is one body and one Spirit—just as you
were called to one hope when you were called.

(EPHESIANS 4:3-4)

Another great experience of the Holy Spirit is the way
He brings unity and fellowship. The world is so full of
substitutes for these two great realities that this is a
needed discovery today. The early Church was
composed of an enormously varied group of men and
women. There were sometimes outspoken disagree-
ments in those first days, but I do not think there was
any fundamental disunity. This unity above freedom to
dissent, above diversity of personality and function,
was the work of the Holy Spirit. No other can give this
power to "disagree without being disagreeable," this
free kind of oneness, this united kind of freedom.

Samuel M. Shoemaker

Thank You for Your patience with us, God,
for we know so little about the unity of the Spirit.

The voice of the Lord strikes with flashes of lightning....
The Lord sits enthroned over the flood; the Lord is enthroned as
King forever. The Lord gives strength to his people;
the Lord blesses his people with peace.

(PSALM 29: 7,10-11)

Thunder
crashing roaring
wakens me.
I get up
to close the window
against the rain.
Lightning tears the sky
for fragmentary moment
I see the yard
wheelbarrow
trees road field
and distant hill.
All is dark again
I return to sleep.
Thank You for the storm
that wakens me
and lightning flash
illumining
things near and far
in usual dark.

Joseph Bayly

Your creation shouts of Your glory,
Lord of thunder and lightning.

I delight greatly in the Lord;
my soul rejoices in my God.

(ISAIAH *61:10*A)

No duty is more urgent than that of returning thanks.

St. Ambrose

To Thee, O God of my fathers, I give thanks;
Thee I praise, who hast in some measure
endued me with wisdom and courage;
and hast showed me that which I requested of Thee,
and hast opened my mouth:
{and hast caused me to be} the work of Thine
hands and the price of Thy Blood;
and the image of Thy countenance, and the
servant of Thy purchase;
and the seal of Thy Name,
and the child of Thine adoption;
and the temple of Thy Spirit,
and a member of Thy Church.

Lancelot Andrewes

I long to see you so that I may impart to you some spiritual gift to make you strong—that is, that you and I may be mutually encouraged by each other's faith.

(ROMANS 1:11-12)

Complying with the law for compulsory military service in Argentina, a fellow showed up at the induction center objecting, "What good would I be? I have no arms!" They put him in the army anyway.

At basic training camp, his commanding officer said, "See that fellow up there on the hill pumping water? Go tell him when the pail is full. He's blind!"

Gifts are given us to build up one another and to enable us to serve and glorify Christ together. The eye cannot say it has no need of the ear. If all were hands, how would we walk? Each part of the body is needed to serve the whole. The exercise of our gift is needed to strengthen other saints. We, in turn, will be helped toward maturity through the gifts of others.

Leslie B. Flynn

I'm grateful, Lord, for the way You encourage me through the gifts of my Christian sisters and brothers.

"How do you know me?" Nathanael asked. Jesus answered,
"I saw you while you were still under the fig tree before Philip
called you." Then Nathanael declared, "Rabbi, you are
the Son of God; you are the King of Israel."

(JOHN 1 : 4 8 - 4 9)

I've always like this passage, ever since as a young semi-nary graduate working with preschoolers I wrote a lesson for them based on it called, "Jesus Always Sees Me." That's another way of talking about the doctrine of omnipresence—that God can be and is everywhere in the created universe at once.

While Jesus did not exercise this attribute at all times, a number of biblical stories show that He was aware of events that took place beyond the range of sight. . . . The preschoolers for whom I wrote didn't care to debate to what extent Jesus surrendered exercise of the attributes of Deity when He took on humanity. But they did care that "Jesus always sees me." They did care that even when Mommy and Daddy were out of sight, Jesus was watching over them. . . . Yes, theology is profound. But relationship with God is far greater than the most profound doctrine. And our relationship to God can be expressed in words just as simple as "I saw you."

Larry Richards

I don't understand how it's possible, but thank You
that You see me wherever I am.

Taste and see that the Lord is good;
blessed is the [one] who takes refuge in him.

(PSALM 34:8)

Complementary to this daily and sometimes laborious service is that experience of God *hitlahavut*, the going out of self, the "taste and see how good God is," that engenders a joy that seems to belong to another realm. The peak moments of ecstasy will be few and brief, but the memory of them abides, and something deep within us says that all the strivings of life are worthwhile because of them. The joy of these moments continues to flow as a deep, abiding current in our lives, to be called forth through devotion and service.

M. Basil Pennington

"My God, and My All." What would I more,
and what greater happiness can I desire, O sweet and
delightful word ... My God and my All ... Thou givest quietness
of heart, and much peace, and pleasant joy.

Thomas à Kempis

I the Lord do not change.

(MALACHI 3:6)

What is there in life to which we can safely commit our trust? We cannot rely on ourselves; we are frail, fragile, finite. We cannot rely on nature. It is fickle—sometimes beautiful, sometimes savage and "red in tooth and claw." Others whom we trust may fail us. Organizations and governments betray their "feet of clay."

But the Lord is always faithful, dependable, immutable.

The Greek mathematician Archimedes asked only for one fixed and immovable point in order to move the whole earth from its place—"so I may have great hopes if I find even the least thing that is unshakably certain." That archimedian point—the basis of all certainty—is the Lord, Christ the Truth! He alone can sustain the whole structure of human knowledge and experience.

Henry Gariepy

All praise to You, Lord Christ,
the unshakable basis of all certainty!

Joseph, a Levite from Cyprus, whom the apostles
called Barnabas (which means Son of Encouragement),
sold a field he owned and brought the money
and put it at the apostles' feet.

(ACTS 4:36)

Joseph helped people so much that the apostles called him "Barnabas, the Son of Encouragement." In the early church confession of Christ made it harder to secure and hold employment. Local believers had to help. Barnabas responded by selling property and surrendering the sale price at the apostles' feet to be used to alleviate temporal needs.

When the disciples were leery of Paul, Barnabas sponsored Paul's cause with such success that the suspected newcomer "was with them coming in and going out at Jerusalem." . . . Though doubtless engaged in some work, Paul had magnificent gifts which Barnabas now encouraged him to use at Antioch. So, Barnabas, with his ability to see potential in people, brought Paul as his helper. Later, without envy on his part, Barnabas recognized the leadership of Paul.

Leslie B. Flynn

Father, I thank You for those in my life who have been
"people of encouragement" to me.

May God himself, the God of peace,
sanctify you through and through.

(1 THESSALONIANS 5:23A)

We are prone to pray about the "big things" in life and forget to pray about the so-called "little things"—until they grow and become big things! Talking to God about *everything* that concerns us and Him is the first step toward victory over worry.

The result is that the "peace of God" guards the heart and the mind. "The peace of God" stands guard over the two areas that create worry—the heart (wrong feeling) and the mind (wrong thinking). When we give our hearts to Christ in salvation, we experience "peace with God" but the "peace of God" takes us a step further into His blessings. This does not mean the absence of trials on the outside, but it does mean a quiet confidence within, regardless of circumstances, people, or things.

Warren Wiersbe

You know how easy it is for me to slide into a pattern
of worry, Lord. Thank You for Your peace and the
quiet confidence Your peace brings.

By day the Lord directs his love, at night his song is with me—
a prayer to the God of my life.

(PSALM 42:8)

By examining as closely and candidly as I could the life that had come to seem to me in many ways a kind of trap or dead-end street, I discovered that it really wasn't that at all. I discovered that if you really keep your eye peeled to it and your ears open, if you really pay attention to it, even such a limited and limiting life as the one I was living on Rupert Mountain opened up onto extraordinary vistas. Taking your children to school and kissing your wife goodbye. Eating lunch with a friend. Trying to do a decent day's work. Hearing the rain patter against the window. There is no event so commonplace but that God is present within it, always hiddenly, always leaving you room to recognize him.

Frederick Buechner

Glory to You, God, for being present
in what often seems the "unglorious."

*And in him you too are being built together
to become a dwelling in which God lives by his spirit.*

(EPHESIANS 2:22)

It is as if within you there was a little log cabin in which you and Christ were very close; in this attitude you go about your business. . . . It means that within yourselves you have made a room, a secluded space. You have built it by prayer. . . . You should be more aware of God than anyone else, because you are carrying within you this utterly quiet and silent chamber. Because you are more aware of God, because you have been called to listen in your inner silence, you can bring God to the street, the party, the meeting, in a very special and powerful way. The power is God's but you have contributed yourself. God has asked you and chosen you to be the carrier of that silent place within yourself.

Catherine de Hueck Doherty

*That Your Spirit actually lives in us Lord—what a wonder!
Thank You for the privilege of being Your dwelling place
in the world.*

*Sing to the Lord a new song, his praise
from the ends of the earth.*

(ISAIAH 42:10A)

To God be the glory—great things He has done!
So loved He the world that He gave us His Son,
Who yielded His life an atonement for sin,
And opened the life–gate that all may go in.

Praise the Lord, praise the Lord,
Let the earth hear His voice!
Praise the Lord, praise the Lord,
Let the people rejoice!
O come to the Father through Jesus the Son,
And give Him the glory—great things He has done.

Fanny J. Crosby

I give You the glory, and praise You in song.

I will praise you, O Lord my God, with all my heart;
I will glorify your name forever. For great is your love
toward me; you have delivered my soul
from the depths of the grave.

(P S A L M   *86:12-13*)

It is said that in a time of great despondency among the first settlers in New England, it was proposed in one of their public assemblies to proclaim a fast. An old farmer arose; spoke of their provoking heaven with their complaints, reviewed their measures, showed that they had much to be thankful for, and moved that instead of appointing a day of fasting, they should appoint a day of thanksgiving. This was done; the custom has been continued ever since.

However great our difficulties, or deep even our sorrow, there is room for thankfulness.

Dwight L. Moody

In spite of troubles that threaten, there is room to be thankful,
and I do thank You, God.

You have made known to me the path of life;
you will fill me with joy in your presence,
with eternal pleasures at your right hand.

(PSALM *16:11*)

After dinner one evening my mother and I were comfortably settled in our living room. . . All at once it happened. My heart overflowed with praise. Silently, I lifted all of it to Him, aware now of His presence . . . *This quiet room, the comforts and the peace of it. No bombs are falling outside. No Gestapo is going to pound on the door . . . By Your mercy and grace, Mother is still with us, the inimitable Christy, so gentle, yet so full of her own kind of ginger. You love her too. Isn't it great that she and I have such rapport that often conversation isn't even necessary! . . . This music, so glorious. It must be pleasing you too. Work for my hands to do, work that I enjoy. You know all about work with the hands. This moment—what delight—what an oasis—in the midst of busy life. . . .* The thankfulness bubbled up and up . . .

Catherine Marshall

Sometimes I'm overwhelmed with the joy
of being Yours, my Lord.

The birds of the air nest by the waters;
they sing among the branches.... How many
are your works, O Lord! In wisdom you made them all;
the earth is full of your creatures.... These all look to you
to give them their food at the proper time.

(P S A L M *104:12,24,27*)

The inherent abundance of the earth is simply amazing. One man has said that if we consider only the amount of food consumed by the birds of the air every day, and how much it would cost if we had to purchase it, the figure is simply staggering. No country in the world has that kind of money. Yet, the small part of God expressed in what we call nature, feeds them every day. When one thinks about it, he cannot but stand in awe of the abundance all about us waiting to be released for the benefit of all earth's creatures.

Norman Elliott

I praise You for the way You have arranged
for the care of nature.

Then the word of the Lord came to Jonah a second time:
"Go to the great city of Nineveh and proclaim to it
the message I give you."

(JONAH 3: 1-2)

When mistakes happen, relax. Expect God to act.
God can make compost out of our failures. He can
give us a second chance, as he gave to the prophet
Jonah. In the Old Testament story we read that even
after Jonah ignored the Lord and did not do what he
wanted, the Lord came to Jonah a second time. The
Lord can intervene and direct a second time or a third
time. He uses all those times to bring about his will.

Bruce Larson

Thank You for not giving up on me, Lord. Thank You
for trying a second and third time, and more.

But you are a shield around me, O Lord,
my Glorious One, who lifts up my head.

(PSALM 3:3)

As his son Absalom led a national revolt against his father, David lapsed into despair: "O Lord, how my adversaries have increased! Many are rising up against me." But then notice how quickly David's attitude changes: "But Thou, O Lord, art a shield about me."

What accounts for David's new courage? I believe that David started to remember God's past faithfulness to him. And such reflection reminded him that God was completely capable and willing to sustain him now.

In the same way, I believe God wants us to have a pool of memories to draw from in times of adversity. Such memories of God's prior faithfulness can relieve anxiety. Specifically, I would suggest that you keep a journal of your prayer requests, making sure to date each request and record the answer to that request.

Robert Jeffress

I remember the many times You've shown Your faithfulness
to me, Father God. I remember with thanksgiving.

All this is from God, who reconciled us to himself through Christ and gave us the ministry of reconciliation: that God was reconciling the world to himself in Christ, not counting men's sins against them. And he has committed to us the message of reconciliation. We are therefore Christ's ambassadors, as though God were making his appeal through us.

(2 CORINTHIANS 5:18-20A)

Think of the news you are ordained to declare. That God has invaded history with power and great glory; that in the day of man's terrible need a second Adam has come forth to the fight and to the rescue; that in the cross the supreme triumph of naked evil has been turned once for all to irrevocable defeat; that Christ is alive now and present through his Spirit; that through the risen Christ there has been let loose into the world a force which can transform life beyond recognition— this is the most momentous message human lips were ever charged to speak. It dwarfs all other truths into insignificance. It is electrifying in its power, shattering in its wonder.

James S. Stewart

I praise You that You've made me Your ambassador, proclaiming an astounding message!

*When Jesus spoke again to the people he said, "I am the light
of the world. Whoever follows me will never walk
in darkness, but will have the light of life."*

(JOHN 8:12)

Every student of astronomy knows that there are two
orders of luminaries. There is that which is its own
source of light. The sun is of this order. Then there is
the luminary which has no light of its own. It catches
and reflects light from another source. The moon is an
example of that kind of luminary. Without the light of
the sun it would be a sterile, dark ball in a midnight
sky. But catching the radiance of the sun, it becomes a
glowing, luminous heavenly body up in our sky. Our
light is a borrowed ray from the Sun of Righteousness.
How wonderful it is that our lives can catch His radiance and reflect it in a darkened world.

Henry Gariepy

*Praise to You, Sun of Righteousness, that my life
can reflect Your radiance.*

But let all who take refuge in you be glad;
let them ever sing for joy. Spread your protection over them,
that those who love your name may rejoice in you.

(PSALM 5:11)

Life really is fun, if we only give it a chance. Countless moments of serendipity are constantly alive to us and inviting us to participate, if we but have eyes to see, ears to hear, and hearts to respond. Everyday life has its own hidden comedy. As John Powell said, "Blessed is he who has learned to laugh at himself, for he shall never cease to be entertained." When we can laugh at ourselves and our own situations and the life around us, it literally produces physiological and chemical changes in our bodies that bring about a greater sense of vitality, health, and even healing.

Tim Hansel

What a great idea, God, to invent laughter!

He does not treat us as our sins deserve or repay us
according to our iniquities. . . for he knows how we
are formed, he remembers that we are dust.

(P S A L M   1 0 3 : 1 0 ,   1 4)

When our dear Lord will one day reach down and
snatch us up—up before Him *blameless* . . . flawless, He
will be no peeved deity, angry because of our failures
and ready to strike us because they were many (Ps.
103:10, 14). . . . You would think it a natural thing for
the Almighty to frown and draw from His records a
legal-size clipboard with your name at the top upon
which would be listed the numerous times you stum-
bled. How depressing a thought! No—a thousand
times, no! God keeps no such records to be used
against you.

He will accept you in that day, being fully aware that
you are but dust . . . and He will escort you into the
presence of His glory BLAMELESS. I invite you to
stop at this moment and think that over. It's not possible to imagine the scene without smiling, seized with
inexpressible joy.

Charles R. Swindoll

Blameless, Lord! Thank You!

COUNT YOUR BLESSINGS

*To him who is able to keep you from falling and to
present you before his glorious presence without fault and
with great joy—to the only God our Savior be glory,
majesty, power and authority, through Jesus Christ our Lord,
before all ages, now and forevermore! Amen.*

(JUDE 24-25)

Grace and gratitude belong together like heaven and
earth. Grace evokes gratitude like the voice an echo.
Gratitude follows grace as thunder follows lightning.

Karl Barth

*Almighty God, Father of all mercies, we, thine unworthy ser-
vants, do give thee most humble and hearty thanks for all thy
goodness and lovingkindness to us, and to all [people]. We bless
thee for our creation, preservation, and all the blessings of this
life; but above all for thine inestimable love in the redemption of
the world by our Lord Jesus Christ; for the means of grace, and
the hope of glory. And we beseech thee, give us that due sense of
all thy mercies, that our hearts may be unfeignedly thankful; and
that we show forth thy praise, not only with our lips, but in our
lives, by giving up ourselves to thy service, and by walking before
thee in holiness and righteousness all our days; through Jesus
Christ our Lord, to whom, with thee and the Holy Ghost, be all
honor and glory, world without end. Amen.*

The General Thanksgiving

Rejoice in the Lord and be glad, you righteous;
sing, all you who are upright in heart!

(PSALM 32:11)

I have found that one of the surest ways of releasing God's joy in my life is to stop frequently to give thanks for the blessings of each day, each week, each month, each year.

When we tally up our blessings, let's not forget the small blessings of each day. . . . Take a sheet of paper and begin by listing the blessings you enjoy this very day. At the top of your list might be your ability to read and your ability to write such a list. Then think of the blessings of health, of talents, of family, of friends, the blessings of your neighborhood, your house, your state, your country. When so many in the world are faced with war and oppression and terror, think of the protection and peace you enjoy. Then begin to work backwards, remembering the blessings of the past week, the past month, the past year. Then let your mind rove back through your life, thinking of those blessings you especially treasure. It would be surprising if at the end of the list you could not write: "The Lord has done great things for me; I am glad."

Ron Klug

Lord, You <u>have</u> done great things for me, and I praise You.

Finally, be strong in the Lord and in his mighty power.

(EPHESIANS 6:10)

Nothing is ever wasted in the kingdom of God. Not one tear, not all our pain, not the unanswered questions or the seemingly unanswered prayers. . . . Nothing will be wasted if we give our lives to God. And if we are willing to be patient until the grace of God is made manifest, whether it takes nine years or ninety, it will be worth the wait.

Rebecca Manley Pippert

O Impatient Ones! Do the leaves say nothing to you as they murmur today? They are not fashioned this spring, but months ago; and the summer just begun will fashion others for another year. At the bottom of every leaf-stem is a cradle, and in it is an infant germ; and the winds will rock it, and the birds will sing to it all summer long, and next season it will unfold. So God is working for you and carrying forward to the perfect development all the processes of our lives.

Henry Ward Beecher

*Thank You for patience, Lord, to trust
that You are at work at Your pace.*

Rejoice with those who rejoice;
mourn with those who mourn.
(ROMANS 12:15)

One evening I was in an hour-long prayer meeting. It was a very special time as we prayed together in small groups. A wonderful binding of hearts takes place when we are focused on the living Christ and sense the power of God's Holy Spirit helping us to pray.

There is a wonderful coming together and a oneness in prayer that is not found in anything else we do. . . . When you have a person or a group with whom you can pray, you have an awareness of the power and the strength and the love and the peace of God that you will find in no other situation.

Roger Palms

Thank You, God, for the rich experience
of praying with other believers.

Like cold water to a weary soul is
good news from a distant land.

(P R O V E R B S 25:25)

There has been an enforced separation from loved ones. Anxiety crowds the mind over their safety and welfare. A long time has elapsed since word has been received from or of them. Then one day comes the surprise and joy of a letter. It brings the "good news from a distant land" that has been long awaited. It cheers the heart. It refreshes, restores, as that drink of cold water.

The Gospel, above all else, is good news from a distant land. It comes from heaven to earth, from God to man. It is to the thirsty soul the most satisfying drink. It satisfies the deep thirst that no earthly spring can quench. When weary of the journey, we drink its life-giving waters and are refreshed, restored, and enabled to go on.

Henry Gariepy

Your Word to me, O God, is like cold water to my thirsty soul.

And surely I will be with you always,
to the very end of the age.

(MATTHEW 28:20B)

Jesus awakens on a grassy slope near Jerusalem. As the first light dawns, the apostles begin to stir; one by one they awake and stretch and yawn. Another day is beginning in their walk with the Master.

It is overwhelming to realize that the apostles were so simply and totally available to the Lord. Despite their limited grasp of his full identity, they followed Jesus and were with him night and day.

When you awake in the morning, Jesus is also there, fully present to you just as he was to the apostles. . . . When you awake tomorrow, look around and you will see Jesus stirring, too, ready to lead you through a day in which he can use you, your work and your talents for his purpose.

Leo Holland

You <u>are</u> here, Jesus—with me throughout this day.

*Keep your lives free from the love of money and
be content with what you have, because God has said,
"Never will I leave you; never will I forsake you."*

(HEBREWS *13:5*)

God is named *Elohim* no fewer than 2,500 times in the Old Testament. *Elohim* means "the God who promises and has the might to keep His promises."

God has promised to never leave us or forsake us. . . When we are caught between work and family, Elohim speaks softly to us, "Follow Me. Keep your word as I have kept Mine." Elohim serves us as both instructor and comforter. We learn from Elohim to follow through on our commitments to our families even when it is not easy. And we learn from Elohim that our fathering God will keep His promises to us, that He is the almighty keeper of His word. As the creator God, He is capable of doing what He has said He will do.

Jack and Jerry Schreur

*Father God, in an uncertain world, thank You
that I can depend on You to keep Your promises.*

*The King will reply,"I tell you the truth, whatever
you did for one of the least of these brothers of mine,
you did it for me."*

(MATTHEW 25:40)

A grateful life is a life in which we come to see that the
Lord himself is the gift. The mystery of ministry is that
the Lord is to be found where we minister. That is
what Jesus tells us when he says: "Insofar as you did this
to one of the least of these brothers of mine, you did it
to me." Our care for people thus becomes the way to
meet the Lord. The more we give, help, support, guide,
counsel, and visit, the more we receive, not just similar gifts, but the Lord himself.

Henri J.M. Nouwen

Giver of gifts, You are my best gift. Now give through me.

How can we thank God enough for you
in return for all the joy we have in the presence
of our God because of you?

(1 THESSALONIANS 3:9)

We invest in other people, for this is what it means to be a true minister of the Gospel. As Paul said, "How can I thank God for the rejoicing that I have because of you, your faith, your growth, and your activity for the Gospel?" And then he said, "Night and day we pray most earnestly that we may see you again and supply what is lacking in your faith." He knew what some of us can still learn—the joy of encouraging, helping, teaching others, and supplying to them what is still lacking. Part of the joy we have in Christ is that we get to pray for each other and help bring one another along to completion in Christ Jesus. No one in Christ is beyond learning. And no one is without a ministry to someone else. All of us have something to invest in another.

Roger Palms

Thank You, Lord, for the joy of seeing others built up in faith.

Since the children have flesh and blood,
he too shared in their humanity.

(H E B R E W S   2 : 1 4 A)

Berakah . . . [translated "blessing"] describes what God does to us and among us . . . God gets down on his knees among us; gets on our level and shares himself with us. He does not reside afar off and send us diplomatic messages, he kneels among us. That posture is characteristic of God. . . Everything we learn about God through Scripture and in Christ tells us that he knows what it is like to change a diaper for the thirteenth time in the day, have a report over which we have worked long and carefully gather dust on somebody's desk for weeks and weeks, find our teaching treated with scorn and indifference by children and youth, discover that the integrity and excellence of our work has been overlooked and the shoddy duplicity of another's rewarded with a promotion. . . God stoops—he kneels to our level and meets us where we are; God stays—he sticks with us through hard times and good, sharing his life with us in grace and peace.

Eugene H. Peterson

You understand, God. Thank You.

Therefore we do not lose heart.
Though outwardly we are wasting away,
yet inwardly we are being renewed day by day.

(2 C O R I N T H I A N S 4 : 16)

Sometimes it is not difficulty that makes me think God will forsake me, but drudgery. There is no Hill Difficulty to climb, no vision given, nothing wonderful or beautiful, just the commonplace day in and day out—can I hear God's say–so in these things?

We have the idea that God is going to do some exceptional thing, that He is preparing and fitting us for some extraordinary thing by and bye, but as we go on in grace we find that God is glorifying Himself here and now, in the present minute. If we have God's say-so behind us, the most amazing strength comes, and we learn to sing in the ordinary days and ways.

Oswald Chambers

I sing in this ordinary day because You are here.
Glorify Yourself through me.

*Now it is God who makes both us and you stand firm
in Christ. He anointed us, set his seal of ownership on us,
and put his Spirit in our hearts as a deposit,
guaranteeing what is to come.*

(2 CORINTHIANS 1:21-22)

A hard day, yes. Rattled and unglued, yes. Unable to cope, no.

How does the life-giving Spirit of the risen Lord manifest Himself on days like that? In our willingness to stand fast, our refusal to run away and escape into self-destructive behavior. Resurrection power enables us to engage in the savage confrontation with untamed emotions, to accept the pain, receive it, take it on board, however acute it may be. And in the process we discover that we are not alone, that we can stand fast in the awareness of present risenness and so become fuller, deeper, richer disciples.

Brennan Manning

*Thank You, Lord. Your life-giving Spirit
makes it possible for me to stand fast.*

Therefore I tell you, whatever you ask for in prayer,
believe that you have received it, and it will be yours.

(M A R K 11:24)

Hudson Taylor, founder of the China Inland Mission, sent out an urgent appeal in 1875 that God would raise up 18 suitable workers that year. By the end of the year 18 new workers came. At Christmas 1877 he asked friends to pray for at least 30 new workers the next year. By the end of next December, 28 new workers had sailed, with several others accepted by the mission and scheduled to follow shortly.

In 1887 news reached England that Hudson Taylor was fervently praying for 100 new missionaries. He said with the gift of faith, "If you showed me a photograph of the whole 100 taken in China, I could not be more sure than I am now." Before the year ended, more than 600 offered themselves for service. After careful evaluation, 102 were finally selected, all sailing by December 29.

Leslie B. Flynn

For encouraging accounts of people of faith,
like Hudson Taylor, I thank You, God.

For he has clothed me with garments of salvation
and arrayed me in a robe of righteousness.

(ISAIAH 61:10B)

The grace of Christ clothes us, as it were, with gorgeous purple and raises us to a dignity that surpasses knowledge.

St. Cyril of Alexandria

I am your servant! Everything I have is yours.
But even as I say that, I know you are serving me more than
I am serving you. At your command all of the resources of heav-
en and earth are at my disposal, and even the angels
help me. Yet you serve me in a way that surpasses
all of this: you promise to give yourself to me.
You are the great Servant of us all.

Thomas à Kempis

Praise be to the God and Father of our Lord Jesus Christ,
who has blessed us in the heavenly realms with every
spiritual blessing in Christ.

(EPHESIANS 1:3)

There are people who deep down are thinking, "God hasn't really blessed me. If God were really blessing me, I wouldn't have these family problems, I wouldn't have these financial needs, I wouldn't be struggling socially. I wouldn't be feeling physical pain."

Then someone says, "But He has blessed you with all spiritual blessings."

"But I can't measure that. What spiritual blessings?"

We really can measure spiritual blessings, but not in the same way we measure everything else. They're there, they're ours, and they are gaining interest. We'll know it the moment we turn from looking at the so-called negatives and start looking at God. Praise opens our eyes to blessing.

Roger Palms

I give You thanks for riches far beyond
my imagination, Father.

Sorrowful, yet always rejoicing;
poor, yet making many rich; having nothing,
and yet possessing everything.

(2 CORINTHIANS 6:10)

The way to deeper knowledge of God is through the lonely valleys of soul poverty and abnegation of all things. The blessed ones who possess the Kingdom are they who have repudiated every external thing and have rooted from their hearts all sense of possessing. These are the "poor in spirit." They have reached an inward state paralleling the outward circumstances of the common beggar in the streets of Jerusalem; that is what the word "poor" as Christ used it actually means. These blessed poor are no longer slaves to the tyranny of things. They have broken the yoke of the oppressor; and this they have done not by fighting but by surrendering. Though free from all sense of possessing, they yet possess all things. "Theirs is the kingdom of heaven."

A.W. Tozer

Jesus, thank You that no matter what happens to my
material possessions, I already have all that really matters.

As far as the east is from the west, so far has
he removed our transgressions from us.

(PSALM 103:12)

Over the years, a number of people have told me,
"God could never forgive me for what I've done."
Ironically, some of these people are Christians. They
believe that Jesus Christ died for them, that His blood
atoned for the sins of humanity. But somehow they feel
that doesn't apply to them.

How plainly can I put it? God *understands*. He knows
the extenuating circumstances, your limits, your weaknesses, the pressures on you. God *cares* deeply about
you. He feels your pain. God *forgives*. He knows your
sins in gruesome detail. And still He loves you. By
Christ's atoning death, your sins have been carted off,
as far as the east is from the west.

David New

What language should I borrow
To thank thee, dearest friend,
For this thy dying sorrow,
Thy pity without end?
O make me thine forever;
And should I fainting be,
Lord, let me never, never
Outlive my love to thee. Amen

Bernard of Clairvaux

To him who loves us and has freed us
from our sins by his blood, and has made us
to be a kingdom and priests to serve his God
and Father—to him be glory and power
for ever and ever! Amen.

(REVELATION 1:5B-6)

Every seven years, the Jews were to observe a "sabbatical year" and allow the land to rest. After seven sabbaticals, or forty-nine years, they were to celebrate the fiftieth year as the "Year of Jubilee." During that year, all debts were canceled, all land was returned to the original owners, the slaves were freed, and everybody was given a fresh new beginning. This was the Lord's way of balancing the economy and keeping the rich from exploiting the poor.

If you have trusted Christ as your Savior, you are living today in a spiritual "Year of Jublilee." You have been set free from bondage; your spiritual debt to the Lord has been paid.

Warren Wiersbe

I celebrate my "Year of Jubilee" with praise to You, Jesus.

In the year that King Uzziah died, I saw the Lord
seated on a throne, high and exalted, and the train of his robe
filled the temple. Above him were seraphs, each with six wings:
With two wings they covered their faces, with two they covered
their feet, and with two they were flying. And they were
calling to one another: "Holy, holy, holy is the Lord Almighty;
the whole earth is full of his glory."

(I S A I A H 6 : 1 - 3)

I love my life supremely because Thou art my life's
sweetness.

Nicholas of Cusa

O Everlasting Light, surpassing all created luminaries:
dart the beams of Thy brightness from above and pene-
trate all the corners of my heart.

Thomas à Kempis

When I think of God, my heart is so filled with joy
that the notes fly off as from a spindle.

Joseph Hayden

Oh Holy One, I can't begin to comprehend Your greatness.
But I can begin to comprehend Your love.

Have you not read what God said to you,
"I am the God of Abraham, the God of Isaac,
and the God of Jacob"? He is not the God
of the dead but of the living.

(M ATTHEW 22:31B-32)

When a stranger thinks of China, he imagines a vague multitude, with faces that look all alike. . . . When God thinks of China, he knows every one of the Chinese by name. . . . He lifts us up from the obscurity of our littleness; he picks us out from the multitude of our fellows; he gives to our lives the dignity of his individual care. The Eternal God calls us every one by name. He is not the God of mankind in the mass; he is the God of *Abraham*, of *Isaac*, and of *Jacob*.

Harry Emerson Fosdick

. . . and of me. You see me. You know my name.
Thank You, God.

If I go up to the heavens, you are there;
if I make my bed in the depths, you are there.
If I rise on the wings of the dawn, if I settle
on the far side of the sea, even there your
hand will guide me, your right hand
will hold me fast.

(PSALM 139:8-10)

Deep faith in our Heavenly Father makes it possible for us to leave the past in his hands. We have sprung from the eternal heart of God, for we are created in his image. The mistakes and sins of our past have been caught up in his love.

We stand in the present, grateful for the rich heritage and lessons of the past, and move confidently toward the future which God holds securely in his hands. We may not know *where* we are going, but we know *with whom* we are journeying. Thus we are set free to live fully in the now. Let us thank God for all that has been, for the miracle of what is, and for the haunting call of what is yet to be.

Lionel A. Whiston

Heavenly Father, thank You for what has been. You were there. Thank You for what is. You are here. Thank You for what is yet to be. You will be with me.

*For I do not want you to be ignorant of the fact, brothers,
that our forefathers were all under the cloud and that they all
passed through the sea.... These things happened to them as
examples and were written down as warnings for us,
on whom the fulfillment of the ages has come.*

(1 CORINTHIANS 10:1,11)

"Everything that was written in the past was written to
teach us," Paul penned. . . How does God react to
dashed hopes? Read the story of Jairus. How does the
Father feel about those who are ill? Stand with him at
the pool of Bethesda. Do you long for God to speak to
your lonely heart? Then listen as he speaks to the
Emmaus-bound disciples. What is God's word for the
shameful? Watch as his finger draws in the dirt of the
Jerusalem courtyard.

He's not doing it just for them. He's doing it for me.
He's doing it for you.

Max Lucado

*Thank You for what was written in the past
to teach and guide me now.*

Peace I leave with you; My peace I give you.
I do not give to you as the world gives.
Do not let your hearts be troubled
and do not be afraid.

(J O H N   1 4 : 2 7)

Although the world is plagued with anxiety, God never intended His children to be overtaken by it. In fact, Jesus Christ left us with a potent antidote to worry: His peace. We appropriate Christ's gift of peace through the attitude of faith. Faith is not a hope or a wish, but it is a confidence that God is going to take care of us.

Most of us have to admit that we are not enjoying the gift of peace that Christ left us. Why? Because we *choose* worry over peace. The moment we are faced with a negative circumstance we can respond in one of two ways. We can choose to worry about the situation, or we can choose to believe that God is in control of this circumstance and will take care of us.

Robert Jeffress

Jesus, I need Your gift of peace. Thank You.

The creation waits in eager expectation for the sons of God to be revealed. For the creation was subjected to frustration, not by its own choice, but by the will of the one who subjected it, in hope that the creation itself will be liberated from its bondage to decay and brought into the glorious freedom of the children of God. We know that the whole creation has been groaning as in the pains of childbirth right up to the present time. Not ony so, but we ourselves, who have the firstfruits of the Spirit, groan inwardly as we wait eagerly for our adoption as sons, the redemption of our bodies.

(ROMANS 8:19-23)

Our creation was a gift, and when evil entered in, grace abounded even more (Rom. 5:20). God reconciled the world and has given everything a new future. A process of healing and reconciliation is under way and will issue in transformation and consummation. It is not an easy process. It was easier for God to create the world than to redeem it now that it is broken. What an art to retrieve clay that was spoiled and reshape it into something lovely! But the power of God makes life new, the alchemy of his grace creates beauty out of ashes.

Clark H. Pinnock and Robert C. Brow

I praise You for retrieving the clay of me and reshaping it for Your glory!

*Dear friends, do not be surprised at the painful trial you are
suffering, as though something strange were happening to you.
But rejoice that you participate in the sufferings of Christ,
so that you may be overjoyed when his glory is revealed.*

(1 PETER 4:12-13)

In time of trouble, say, "First, He brought me here. It is
by His will I am in this strait place; in that I will rest."
Next, "He will keep me here in His love, and give me
grace in this trial to behave as His child." Then say,
"He will make the trial a blessing, teaching me lessons
He intends me to learn, and working in me the grace
He means to bestow." And last, say, "In His good time
He can bring me out again. How and when, He
knows." Therefore, say, "I am here (1) by God's
appointment, (2) in His keeping, (3) under His training, (4) for His time."

Andrew Murray

*Father God, how good You are to use painful experiences
to teach us Your grace-full lessons.*

For the Lord himself will come down from heaven,
with a loud command, with the voice of the archangel and
with the trumpet call of God, and the dead in Christ
will rise first. After that, we who are still alive and are left
will be caught up with them in the clouds to meet the Lord
in the air. And so we will be with the Lord forever.
Therefore encourage each other with these words.

(1 THESSALONIANS 4:16-18)

And I, even in my captivity, am still free. Under the dirt of my sins I still bear the image and likeness of my Creator. I don't have to wallow helplessly and hopelessly. If I was free to sin, I am also free to repent. It's so simple. I have only to reach out my hand from my grave, from my coffin, from the body of my death, and the Life-Giver will lift me up. With one powerful pull, the Mighty One will lead me out into the endless dance of that Easter Day which knows no evening.

A Priest of the Byzantine Church

Life-Giver, thank You for lifting me up to endless life,
endless dance.

*I have told you this so that my joy may be in you
and that your joy may be complete.*

(JOHN 15:11)

Problems arose for translators when they encountered certain words for which there is no corresponding word in the Eskimo language. For example, there is a passage which tells us that the disciples are filled with joy on seeing Jesus. But since there is no word for "joy" in the Eskimo language, the translators had to find another way to express the meaning of the passage.

They discovered that one of the most joyful times for an Eskimo family is when the sled dogs are fed in the evening. The dogs come barking and yelping, running about and wagging their tails furiously. The children are squealing with delight. It is altogether a "joyous" time.

The translators decided to use that daily event. As a result, when the passage is translated back into English, it reads: "When the disciples saw Jesus, they wagged their tails."

John C. Maxwell

Jesus, You are my joy!

Dear friends, let us love one another, for love comes from God.
Everyone who loves has been born of God and knows God.

(1 JOHN 4:7)

God not only loves us more and better than we can ever love ourselves—but God loved us before we loved, or could love, Him. God's love of us rendered possible and actual our love of God.

Friedrich von Hugel

Thank you for children
brought into being
because we loved.
God of love
keep us loving
so that they
may grow up whole
in love's overflow.

Joseph Bayly

It is good to praise the Lord and make music to your name,
O Most High, to proclaim your love in the morning
and your faithfulness at night.

(PSALM 92:1-2)

Render then thanks to Him always, recognising Him as good and wise and loving, no less when some things are denied you than if they are granted to you; remaining steadfast whatever happens, and joyful in an humble submission to His divine providence.

Lorenzo Scupoli

Great is thy faithfulness, O God my Father,
There is no shadow of turning with thee;
Thou changest not, thy compassions they fail not;
As thou hast been thou forever wilt be.

Great is thy faithfulness!
Morning by morning new mercies I see;
All I have needed thy hand hath provided;
Great is thy faithfulness, Lord, unto me!

Thomas Obediah Chisholm

Greet Rufus, chosen in the Lord, and his mother,
who has been a mother to me, too.

(ROMANS *16:13*)

One day a middle-aged man told me who had made the greatest impact on his life. It was a shoe repairman who lived in his town when he was a little boy. Mr. Coffman didn't just repair shoes. He was a listener to everyone, especially to children. He had time for them when they came by his shop to talk. After he retired, Mr. Coffman was a listener then too. He might be sharpening a saw, but he had time to listen. He might be standing by his car, but he didn't just drive off; he had time to listen.

Mr. Coffman never went to college, he wasn't counted as a world leader, but he had a lot of love. Mr. Coffman had time for people—little boys and grownups too.

Roger Palms

I am so grateful, Lord, for the people who have listened—
really listened—to me.

Oh, the depth of the riches of the wisdom and knowledge
of God! How unsearchable his judgments, and his paths
beyond tracing out! ... For from him and through him
and to him are all things. To him be the glory forever!
Amen.

(ROMANS 11:33,36)

God alone is able by himself to put the soul into a
more blessed, comfortable and happy condition than
can the whole world; yea, and more than if all the
created happiness of all the angels of heaven did dwell
in one man's bosom. I cannot tell what to say. . . . The
life, the glory, the blessedness, the soul-satisfying
goodness that is in God, are beyond all expression.

John Bunyan

Sometimes words fail me, God and I just sit
in Your presence in quiet thanksgiving.

Delight yourself in the Lord; trust in him and he will do this:
He will make your righteousness shine like the dawn,
the justice of your cause like the noonday sun. Be still before
the Lord and wait patiently for him.

(PSALM 37:4-7A)

Not many months after my conversion, having a leisurely afternoon, I retired to my own chamber to spend it largely in communion with God. Well do I remember that occasion. How in the gladness of my heart I poured out my soul before God; and again and again confessing my grateful love to Him who had done everything for me . . . I besought Him to give me some work to do for Him, as an outlet for love and gratitude; some self-denying service, no matter what it might be, however trying or however trivial; something with which He would be pleased, and that I might do for Him who had done so much for me. . . . The presence of God became unutterably real and blessed; and though but a child under sixteen, I remember stretching myself on the ground, and lying there silent before Him with unspeakable awe and unspeakable joy.

J. Hudson Taylor

It's so often in the blessed stillness, Lord,
that Your voice comes through to me.

Now Moses was tending the flock of Jethro his father-in-law, the priest of Midian, and he led the flock to the far side of the desert and came to Horeb, the mountain of God.

(EXODUS 3:1, KJV)

It is always on the backside of the desert that we come to the mountain of God—on the backside of the desert of self, at the end of our own dreams and ambitions and plans.

Poor Moses had made quite a come-down from the courts of Egypt to the desert of Midian. He carried in his hand only a shepherd's rod, fit symbol of his humiliation. God demanded that he cast even that to the ground. And when he took it up again it became henceforth the "rod of God!"

If God has brought you to the backside of the desert, if you are reduced, as it were, to a shepherd's rod, cast even that gladly at His feet and He will restore it to you the rod of God—and with it you shall work wonders in His Name so long as you "endure as seeing Him Who is invisible."

Vance Havner

Thank You for being there—on the backside of the deserts of my life—encouraging me to trust You again.

Come to me, all you who are weary and burdened,
and I will give you rest.

(MATTHEW *11:28*)

As evening drew nigh, and our little fellow had played until he was tired, I noticed that he drew closer and closer to his mother. At last he found the place he was longing for, mother's lap. He did not have a great deal to say either. He simply lay there, and let his mother caress him to sleep.

We, too, become tired, deadly tired, of ourselves, of others, of the world, of life, of everything! Then it is blessed to know of a place where we can lay our tired head and heart, our heavenly Father's arms, and say to him "I can do no more. And I have nothing to tell you. May I lie here a while and rest? Everything will soon be well again if I can only rest in your arms a while."

O. Hallesby

I am grateful for Your loving arms, Heavenly Father.
There I can truly rest.

*All the Israelites grumbled against Moses and Aaron,
and the whole assembly said to them,"If only we had died
in Egypt! Or in this desert! … Then Moses and Aaron fell
facedown … and said to the entire Israelite assembly,
"The land we passed through and explored is exceedingly good. If
the Lord is pleased with us, he will lead us into that land, a land
flowing with milk and honey, and will give it to us.*

(NUMBERS 14:2, 5A, 7-8)

God is still giving His people tasks that, in the world's
terms, seem doomed to faiure. A country lawyer in
Americus, Georgia, heard the word of the Lord about
twenty years ago. Millard Fuller felt God was asking
him to do something about the one billion people in
the world who have inadequate housing, or no housing
at all. I knew Millard in the days when he got that
vision, and I tended to write him off as an impractical
dreamer. Subsequently, the organization called Habitat
for Humanity was born, and tens of thousands of
homes have already been built or improved by means
of interest-free loans and volunteer labor. Thanks to
God's caring people, this impossible mission is becoming more and more possible.

Bruce Larson

*Thank You for giving us impossible dreams
and then helping us make them come true.*

The fear of the Lord is the beginning of wisdom,
and knowledge of the Holy One is understanding.

(PROVERBS 9:10)

The "fear of the Lord" isn't being scared at all. In most Old Testament texts what it means is simply to have respect for God; to be fully aware and in awe of the fact that He is living and present.

This, the fact that we take God's existence and His presence into account when thinking about any issue or making any decision, is "fear of the Lord." And this is the beginning of knowledge. If we take God into account, we look to Him for guidance. And we find it.

Larry Richards

What a blessing to be among those who fear You, God,
and look to You for wisdom.

And he will be called Wonderful Counselor.

(ISAIAH 9:6)

Life is often perplexing, bewildering, complex, prob-
lematic, disconcerting. We have an inescapable need
for the Divine Counselor.

A counselor is one who advises, instructs, and guides
in directing the judgment and conduct of another. He
is involved in the intimacies of life, directing it
through its crises and critical periods. A counselor
needs to be close, accessible. Jesus Christ is as close as
the whisper of a prayer. He is always available, never
away or too busy. A counselor must have a good
knowledge of the person to be counseled. Jesus Christ
knows and understands us better than we know
ourselves. We may with confidence bring to Him the
hurts, the failures, the deep needs and aspirations of
our lives. For Christ is the Counselor par excellence.
He is the Wonderful Counselor.

Henry Gariepy

Jesus, You are as close as the whisper of a prayer.
You are my Wonderful Counselor.

The Lord is good, a refuge in times of trouble.
He cares for those who trust in him.

(N A H U M *1:7*)

After the war Corrie ten Boom knew God wanted her to go to the United States to relate her experiences. With $50 in her purse, the maximum permitted by her government, and two borrowed blank checks, she landed among the skyscrapers of New York City.

After staying a week in the New York YMCA, Corrie was informed by the clerk that she could stay no longer. Corrie replied that the Lord had another room for her, though she did not know the address. The clerk looked puzzled, then suddenly recalled that a letter had arrived for Corrie. Reading the letter, Corrie told the clerk to send her suitcases to a certain address on 109th Street. When the clerk asked why she hadn't known before where to send them, Corrie replied that she got the address from the letter. A woman who had heard her speak that week had written to offer her son's room while he was in Europe. The clerk at the desk was amazed.

Leslie B. Flynn

Praise to You, Lord, my refuge. Your loving care is amazing.

*Praise be to the God and Father of our Lord Jesus Christ,
the Father of compassion and the God of all comfort.*

(2 CORINTHIANS 1:3)

Eva Prior is seventy-three years old and legally blind.
She can't drive or read or watch television and, she
says impishly, "I can't even see my own face in the
mirror. But that might be a blessing in disguise!" That
doesn't stop her. She says, "Even with this difficulty,
the Lord has not laid me aside. I have had the wonderful joy of discipling new Christians and sometimes
older Christians who have been on the way for a long
time but are struggling. They come to my home for
discipling. It has been a wonderful joy to me because
they're all ages and from different walks of life. God
has brought them to me. I do believe that this has been
even a greater blessing to me than to them."

Roger Palms

Lord, thank You for the blessing of blessing others.

Then the King shall say to those on his right, "Come,
you who are blessed by my Father; take your inheritance,
the kingdom prepared for you since the creation of the world.
For I was hungry and you gave me something to eat,
I was thirsty and you gave me something to drink,
I was a stranger and you invited me in."

(MATTHEW 25:34-35)

Lord of all pots and pans and things
    Since I've no time to be
A saint by doing lovely things
    Or watching late with thee,
Or dreaming in the dawnlight,
    Or storming heaven's gates,
Make me a saint by getting meals
    And washing up the plates.

Thou who didst love to give men food
    In room or by the sea,
Accept this service that I do—
    I do it unto thee.

Author Unknown

It gives me joy to know that the most ordinary service
to another is not ordinary to You.

Because of the Lord's great love we are not consumed,
for his compassions never fail. They are new every morning;
great is your faithfulness.

(LAMENTATIONS 3:22-23)

With the earliest birds I will make one more singer in the great concert-hall of God. I will not want more rest, or a longer time to myself to consider all my troubles, I will give my best time, the first hour of the day, to the praise of my God.

Charles H. Spurgeon

A Christian is more music
    When he prays,
Than spheres, or angel's praises be,
    In panegyric alleluias.

John Donne

You awaken us to delight in your praise; for you have made us
for yourself, and our hearts are restless until they rest in you.

Augustine

*In love he presdestined us to be adopted as his sons
through Jesus Christ, in accordance with his pleasure
and will—to the praise of his glorious grace,
which he has freely given us in the One he loves.*

(EPHESIANS 1:5-6)

We might at first think it curious that God so often uses suffering to make our lives "to the praise of His glory," as it says in Ephesians. I mean, aren't there better ways we can glorify God—or at least easier ones?

But do you know what God says to us? "If you can praise and glorify Me in *this* circumstance, My child, you can glorify Me in anything."

In other words, whenever a Christian is found faithful in affliction, repaying good for evil, returning love for abuse, holding steadfast through suffering, or loving in the middle of loneliness or grief . . . the Lord receives the truest, brightest, most radiant kind of glory possible.

Joni Eareckson Tada

*Thank You, God, that our suffering is useful—
that it can bring You glory. May it be so.*

Therefore I tell you, do not worry about your life,
what you will eat or drink; or about your body,
what you will wear. Is not life more important than food,
and the body more important than clothes?

(MATTHEW 6:25)

If what we have we receive as a gift, and if what we have is to be cared for by God, and if what we have is available to others, then we will possess freedom from anxiety. "This is the inward reality of simplicity."

. . . To receive what we have as a gift from God is the first inner attitude of simplicity. We work but we know that it is not our work that gives us what we have. We live by grace even when it comes to "daily bread." . . . What we have is not the result of our labor, but of the gracious care of God. When we are tempted to think that what we own is the result of our personal efforts, it takes only a little drought or a small accident to show us once again how radically dependent we are for everything.

Richard J. Foster

Lord, You call me to simplicity. Thank You that in that call
is the promise of Your care for my physical needs.

I am the Bread of Life.

(JOHN 6:35)

The multitude had witnessed the miracleof the feeding of the 5,000 with the five loaves and two fishes. To escape the press of the crowd, Jesus retired to a mountain and then crossed the lake to the other side. The people followed Him by ship. Their enquiries revealed that they were still looking for His miraculous loaves. However, Jesus pointed to the Giver and said, "I am the Bread of Life."

In essence, Jesus said that what bread was to the physical life, He was to the soul.

Bread is needed regularly for its nourishing value. Only Christ, the Bread of Life, can satisfy the deepest hunger and yearning of the soul.

Henry Gariepy

Bread of life, You alone satisfy my soul's deepest hungers.

But to each of us grace has been given
as Christ apportioned it.

(EPHESIANS 4:7)

Grace is free, but it certainly isn't cheap. You may have read the story of David Rothenberg a few years ago. His father, in a fit of rage, went into David's room, poured kerosene all over the room and all over the tiny boy, and lit him on fire. In God's difficult grace, David somehow lived through it, though ninety-five percent of his body was covered with third-degree burns. It is estimated that David will have approximately 5,000 operations in his lifetime. Each year they have to open him up so that he can grow. Along with a few saints and poets, David Rothenberg is aware of the greatest miracle of all: LIFE ITSELF. At the age of 7, he had the audacity to say:

"I am alive!
I am alive!
I am alive!

I didn't miss out on living! and that is wonderful enough for me."

Tim Hansel

Thank You for the miracle of life itself. Thank You
for sufficient grace to live it.

96

But thanks be to God! He gives us the victory
through our Lord Jesus Christ.

(1 CORINTHIANS 15:57)

All growth in the spiritual life is connected with the clearer insight into what Jesus is to us. The more I realize that Christ must be all to me and in me, that all in Christ is indeed for me, the more I learn to live the real life of faith, which, dying to self, lives wholly in Christ. The Christian life is no longer the vain struggle to live right, but the resting in Christ and finding strength in Him as our life, to fight the fight and gain the victory of faith.

Andrew Murray

Come, Thou long-expected Jesus,
Born to set Thy people free.
From our fears and sins release us;
Let us find our rest in Thee.
Israel's Strength and Consolation,
Hope of all the earth Thou art;
Dear Desire of every nation,
Joy of every longing heart!

Charles Wesley

*When Christ came as high priest of the good things that
are already here, he went through the greater and more perfect
tabernacle that is not man–made, that is to say, not a part of this
creation. He did not enter by means of the blood of goats and
calves; but he entered the Most Holy Place once for all by his own
blood, having obtained eternal redemption.*

(HEBREWS 9:11-12)

When Jesus was crucified, perhaps the most significant happening went almost unnoticed, for it must have been quickly repaired by the shocked priests and Levites who cared for the temple. There a thick, woven curtain was miraculously torn from top to bottom. That curtain isolated the holy of holies, the inner room where once a year the high priest entered to make atonement for Israel's sins.

The writer of Hebrews tells us that the curtain was symbolic, and showed that as yet no one had direct or immediate access to God. Sin still kept humanity from God's presence. So the tearing of that curtain announced a new era! The way into the holiest was now open. Through the death of Christ, forgiven sinners have direct and immediate access to Israel's God.

Larry Richards

*Holy God, I bow before You in thanksgiving for Jesus Christ who
has given me direct access to Your presence.*

*Then Jesus told his disciples a parable to show them
that they should always pray and not give up.*

(LUKE 18:1)

I can take my telescope and look millions of miles into
space, but I can lay it aside and go into my room, shut
the door, get down on my knees in earnest prayer, and
see more of heaven and get closer to God than I can
assisted by all the telescopes and material agencies on
earth.

Sir Isaac Newton

Prayer is such an important power. In the concentra-
tion camp, seven hundred of us lived in a room built
for two hundred people. We were all dirty, nervous and
tense. One day a horrible fight broke out amongst the
prisoners. Betsie began to pray aloud. It was if a storm
laid down, until at last all was quiet. Then Betsie said,
"Thank you, Father." A tired old woman was used by
the Lord to save the situation for seven hundred fellow
prisoners through her prayers.

Corrie ten Boom

*What a privilege to be able to communicate with You,
God my Heavenly Father!*

Therefore, as God's chosen people, holy and dearly loved,
clothe yourselves with compassion, kindness,
humility, gentleness and patience.

(COLOSSIANS 3:12)

A pastor went to dinner at the home of one of his church families. Several other families were there too. As the families sat down and ate dinner, the pastor noticed that the parents were unusually strict with their 5-year-old daughter. Maybe, he thought, they just want her to be on her best behavior for company.

When dinner was almost over, the little girl knocked over her milk. Fearfully, she looked up at her parents. The parents seemed frozen. . . . After a rather long silence, the pastor purposely knocked over his almost-finished drink. Another couple knocked over their glasses as well. The anger on the faces of the parents slowly melted away and turned to a smile. They both reached out and knocked over their drinks as well! The whole group broke out in hysterical laughter and had a wonderful evening, because of the compassion of the pastor for a 5-year-old girl.

John C. Maxwell

Thank You for the people I know
who are filled with compassion.

Therefore, my dear friends, as you have always obeyed—
not only in my presence, but now much more in my absence—
continue to work out your salvation with fear and trembling, for
it is God who works in you to will and to act according
to his good purpose.

(PHILIPPIANS 2:12-13)

The more mistakes I make as an adult, the easier it is for me to recompute some past experiences. Now I know, for example, from personal experience of being the father of four children, that even though I love my children, I do not always have the capacity to communicate my love to them. During those times I'm sure my children question their relationship with me. At least I would expect them to feel inadequate or rejected because that's the way I often felt.

Adults have a tremendously powerful influence on little children. Just by being who we are we automatically influences our children and gives them raw materials out of which they create their values, attitudes, and life goals. How frightening! How exciting! Thank God for his ability to use these relationships for ultimate good! Often I thank him for his tremendous ability to love and guide our children in spite of, and because of, their parents.

Hal Edwards

God, I'm grateful that You continue Your business of
loving iand guiding even when I bungle relationships
with the most important people in my life.

I have become like a portent to many, but you are
my strong refuge. My mouth is filled with your praise,
declaring your splendor all day long.

(PSALM 71:7-8)

I am discovering deeper thanks, or perhaps understanding more what giving thanks is all about, as I
experience life in more profound dimensions.

I've been thinking more too about the countless
millions who are more justified than me in keeping
their thanksgiving in. Those whose children cry at
night from pain, those whose parents die too soon.

When the world seems devoid of hope, it is hard to
give thanks. Realistically, I cannot blame them. Yet, I
hear of many who faithfully stay together helping one
another, who, despite living in the streets and eating
the discards of others, sacrifice what they have so
others may survive. For these I give thanks.

Oh, the miracle of thanksgiving brought to us in the lessons of life.
Praise and majesty be yours, Lord. For the healing of thanksgiv-
ing, thank you. Amen.

Thomas G. Pettepiece

You turned my wailing into dancing; you removed my sackcloth and clothed me with joy, that my heart may sing to you and not be silent. O Lord my God, I will give you thanks forever.

(PSALM 30:11-12)

Helen Keller suffered an illness at eighteen months which left her completely blind and deaf. For five years she was isolated from the world and alone in darkness. Then with the help of Anne Sullivan, Helen fought back against her handicap. She never pitied herself; she never gave up. She once said, "The marvelous richness of human experience would lose something of rewarding joy if there were no limitations to overcome. The hilltop hour would not be half so wonderful if there were not dark valleys to traverse."

David Jeremiah

It's true, Lord, those dark valleys do make the hilltops glorious!

*For Christ's love compels us, because we are convinced
that one died for all, and therefore all died. And he died for all,
that those who live should no longer live for themselves
but for him who died for them and was raised again.*

(2 CORINTHIANS 5:14-15)

The way we treat others reveals what we think God is like. Imagine the implications this has for evangelism! The way we treat others is critical. People will understand as much of the love of God as they see in our own lives. The first Bible many people will read will be your life.

We are called, therefore, to mirror the love of God—a love that is so extravagant that we must never keep it to ourselves. We must spread it around. It is not a mushy love, all sentiment and no action. Jesus' love drove him deeply into the lives of people. He cared for their wholeness. . . . Jesus cared for people as he found them. So must we care for their wholeness—spiritual, social, psychological, you name it.

Rebecca Manley Pippert

*It's a privilege, Lord, to be Your representative to my world.
It's also a responsibility I wouldn't want to tackle without
Your promised guidance.*

Therefore I glory in Christ Jesus in my service to God.

(ROMANS 15:17)

I spoke with a woman who admitted that she had a good life. She had a loving husband, two darling children, a comfortable house, and a decent business. "This is too good," she told me. "I keep waiting for something to go wrong. God can't let me have it this good. Eventually He has to make me suffer."

My advice to this woman, and others like her, is simple. Don't worry. Do all you can to share your blessings with others—*but enjoy what God gives you.* Someday He may call you to suffer for Him. He may bring trials your way, but He will also give you the strength to deal with those trials. And you will find joy even in those difficult times. So find the joy here too.

David New

God, give us wider vision
to see and understand
That both the sun and showers
are gifts from Thy great hand.

Helen Steiner Rice

· COUNT YOUR BLESSINGS ·

The Lord lives! Praise be to my Rock!
Exalted be God my Savior!

(PSALM 18:46)

Praise the Lord.
Praise Him in the Rockies
riding mountain trails.
Praise Him
beside tumbling
rushing
rocky
white capped stream.
Praise Him
in high meadow
still forest.
Praise Him on the Cape
eating lobster, clams
walking rainswept beach
barefoot.
Praise Him on Mount Baker
holding ski rope
going uphill
then down.
Praise Him in the snowfall.
Praise Him in the lodge
sitting by the fire

looking out at stars.
Praise Him at the desk
phoning
writing
meeting
planning.
Praise Him in high places
and in low
in excitement
and monotony.
I will sing to the Lord
as long as I live.
I will be glad in the Lord
in the Lord.

Joseph Bayly

In him we have redemption through his blood,
the forgiveness of sins, in accordance with the riches
of God's grace that he lavished on us with all wisdom
and understanding.

(EPHESIANS 1:7-8)

Lavished—did you know that word is in the Bible? Paul writes about God's grace which He freely bestowed on us, "that he lavished on us."

How much more could we want? His riches—not just freely given but lavished upon us. And if we're that rich with His grace, His unmerited favor, His gifts, what could we possibly lack?

Shut your eyes and picture it . . . not just a free pouring out of His grace upon us but a lavishing of God's grace.

Roger Palms

For Your rich grace, God, <u>lavished</u> upon us, thank You!

Now the body is not made up of one part but of many.

(1 CORINTHIANS 12:14)

A well-known conductor was holding a rehearsal one night with a vast array of musicians and a hundred-voice choir. The mighty chorus rang out with peal of organ, blare of horns, and clashing of cymbals. Far back in the orchestra the piccolo player thought, "In all this din, it doesn't matter what I do." Suddenly the conductor stopped the music, flinging up his hands. All became quiet. Someone, he knew, had failed to play his instrument. The shrill note of the piccolo had been missed.

Just as many notes are needed to make harmony, and many colors to make a painting, so many gifts are essential for the functioning of the body of Christ. Every child of God has received one or more gifts to be used for the upbuilding of the church.

Leslie B. Flynn

There are times when I look with disgust at my puny gift, Lord. Then You remind me that every gift is equal in Your sight.

But you are a chosen people, a royal priesthood, a holy nation,
a people belonging to God, that you may declare the praises of
him who called you out of darkness into his wonderful light.

(1 PETER 2:9)

Legend tells of the beautiful Helen of Troy, over whom many battles were fought. When the army returned to Greece, after one of the battles, Helen was not on any of the ships. Menelaus went to try to find her, at great personal peril. He finally found her in a seaport village, suffering from amnesia and living as a prostitute in rags, dirt, shame, and dishonor. Menelaus looked at her and called, "Helen." Her head turned. "You are Helen of Troy!" he said. And with those words, her back straightened and the royal look came back. She remembered who she was She recalled her destiny.

We are destined to be children of the King. When we respond to God's invitation, we rise up to our noble heritage and the honor God has chosen for us. God's call is to greatness, to immortality, to our eternal destiny.

Henry Gariepy

God, my King, thank You for reminding me
of my true identity as a royal child.

I will praise you with the harp for your faithfulness,
O my God; I will sing praise to you with the lyre,
O Holy One of Israel.

(PSALM 71:22-23)

You have given me a special insight into the sweetness of your love: you gave me my life; when I wandered far away, you brought me back again to serve you; you wanted me to love you.

You are a waterfall of unceasing love! What shall I say about you? How can I forget you? You thought of me even when I was lost and desperate. You have been merciful beyond my wildest dream. You have been good to me far above anything I deserve.

Thomas à Kempis

A Zaddick once cried from the depth of his heart: "Would I could love the best of men as tenderly as God loves the worst."

The Hasidic Anthology

Your love, Oh God, is unconditional and infinitely tender.

For I am convinced that neither death nor life,
neither angels nor demons, neither the present nor the future,
nor any powers, neither height nor depth, nor anything else
in all creation, will be able to separate us from the love of God
that is in Christ Jesus our Lord.

(ROMANS 8:38-39)

I am the friend of Jesus. The Resurrected One is victorious and I stand within His sphere of power. Once more it is His "alien" life with which I am in fellowship and which brings me through everything and receives me on the other side of the gloomy grave. It is not the intrinsic quality of my soul nor something supposedly immortal within me that brings me through. No, it is this Wanderer who marches at my side as Lord and Brother and who can no more abandon me on the other side than He could let me out of His hand here on this side of the grave.

Helmut Thielicke

Jesus, my Lord, my heart bursts with gratitude that You will
never let me out of Your hand—now and forever.

But grow in the grace and knowledge of our Lord and Savior
Jesus Christ. To him be glory both now and forever! Amen.

(2 P E T E R 3 : 1 8)

Now this text exactly expresses what we believe to be
God's will for us, and what we also believe He has
made it possible for us to experience. We accept, in
their very fullest meaning, all the commands and
promises concerning our being no more children, and
our growing up into Christ in all things. . . . We rejoice
that we need not continue always to be babes, needing
milk, but that we may, by reason of use and development, become such as have need of strong meat, skill-
ful in the word of righteousness, and able to discern
both good and evil. And none would grieve more than
we at the thought of any finality in the Christian life
beyond which there could be no advance.

Hannah Whitall Smith

Thank You that, like trees and flowers, our souls are meant to
grow and develop and bring You glory.

I praise you because I am fearfully and wonderfully made;
your works are wonderful, I know that full well.

(PSALM 139:14)

For we must know that we are not through growing, developing; that man is not finished; but that also there is inherent in life itself that which places limitations upon us.

Suppose a tree couldn't stop growing; suppose your feet couldn't stop growing. But just grew on and on and there were nothing you could do about it. It is like a figure in Zarathustra . . . the man who had the ear lobe that extended from his head down to the ground—an ear lobe growing and growing, which apparently couldn't stop. It is a wonderful thing that inherent in the life process are limitations, so that though new things start growing, old things also stop growing.

Howard Thurman

God, You thought of everything when You created the earth
and its inhabitants. When we don't mess it up,
Your handiwork operates perfectly.

*Whoever can be trusted with very little
can also be trusted with much.*

(LUKE 16:10A)

The little duties, the details that make a difference, often separate expedience from excellence.

Jesus sanctified human toil working in the carpenter shop for the better part of His life. Then, shaking the wood shavings from His tunic for the last time, He said, "I must do the work of Him who sent me." He spent Himself in toil for the accomplishment of His sacred task.

Our work, when done to please God, becomes not a drag but a delight, not a burden but a blessing, not a frustration but a fulfillment. How deprived we would be if life were all leisure with no opportunity to be productive and contributive to our community and others.

Henry Gariepy

*Thank You for work to do. Thank You for the fulfillment
I experience when I see that even the most usual task
can glorify You.*

*Judas and Silas, who themselves were prophets, said much
to encourage and strengthen the brothers.*

(ACTS 15:32)

Have you ever spent time with someone who could give you ninety-three reasons why a problem can't be solved? Have you ever been around someone who has all sorts of elaborate methods for justifying why the situation is impossible?

Lack of encouragement and ingratitude seem to go together. People who are truly thankful for life will usually be supportive and encouraging. The word *encouragement* means "to put courage into," and since life is often notoriously difficult, we need all the encouragement we can get. Author Jean Houston says, "Perhaps encouragement is the greatest and single most powerful gift that God has ever given us. Nothing seems to impact our lives as much as encouragement."

Tim Hansel

*For those people who always seem to have a word
of encouragement, thank You, Lord.*

Pray also for me, that whenever I open my mouth, words may
be given me so that I will fearlessly make known the mystery
of the gospel, for which I am an ambassador in chains.

(EPHESIANS 6:19-20A)

God often has hidden purposes in the adversity He
allows. Several letters in the New Testament are called
Prison Epistles. Paul wrote these letters, including the
Letter to the Philippians, while he was incarcerated.
The Book of Revelation was penned by the Apostle
John while he was in exile on the isle of Patmos. It was
in prison that John Bunyan saw the great vision that
later became the immortal *Pilgrim's Progress*. The prisons of our lives can often become places of great
opportunity and ministry.

David Jeremiah

My Father, thank You that though Your purposes are
not known to us, You can and do use the difficult times
to accomplish Your purposes.

O Lord, our Lord, how majestic is your name in all the earth!
You have set your glory above the heavens.

(PSALM 8:1)

Joyful, joyful, we adore thee,
  God of glory, Lord of love;
Hearts unfold like flowers before thee,
  Opening to the sun above.
Melt the clouds of sin and sadness,
  Drive the dark of doubt away;
Giver of immortal gladness
  Fill us with the light of day.

All thy works with joy surround thee,
  Earth and heaven reflect thy rays,
Stars and angels sing around thee,
  Center of unbroken praise.
Field and forest, vale and mountain,
  Flowery meadow, flashing sea,
Chanting bird and flowing fountain,
  Call us to rejoice in thee.

Henry Van Dyke

I will sing to the Lord all my life; I will sing praise to my God as long as I live.

(PSALM 104:33)

To be grateful is to recognize the love of God in everything He has given us—and He has given us everything. Every breath we draw is a gift of His love, every moment of existence is a gift of grace, for it brings with it immense graces from Him. Gratitude therefore takes nothing for granted, is never unresponsive, is constantly awakening to new wonder and to praise of the goodness of God. For the grateful man knows that God is good, not by hearsay but by experience. And that is what makes all the difference.

Thomas Merton

Yes, Lord, I know You are good because You have shown Your goodness to me.

Take the helmet of salvation and the sword of the Spirit,
which is the word of God.

(EPHESIANS 6:24)

He looks! and ten thousands of angels rejoice,
And myriads wait for his word;
He speaks! and eternity, filled with his voice,
Reechoes the praise of the Lord.

Joseph Swain

Lord, arm me with Thy Spirit's might,
Since I am called by Thy great name:
In Thee my wandering thoughts unite,
Of all my works be Thou the aim:
Thy love attend me all my days,
And my sole business be Thy praise.

John Wesley

COUNT YOUR BLESSINGS

...and into an inheritance that can never perish, spoil or fade—
kept in heaven for you

(1 PETER 1:4)

In Peter's Epistle we read of an inheritance which is imperishable, undefiled, and will not fade away. A reserved inheritance that already has your name on it. It won't perish because it's imperishable. It won't be something defiled because it can't be defiled. It will not fade away. It will always be there.

And why is this inheritance reserved? We have a living hope through the resurrection of Jesus Christ from the dead, because according to His great mercy He has caused us to be born again. Peter wouldn't say it if God hadn't done it. A reservation in heaven! An inheritance—imperishable! Undefiled! Eternal! So relax. You've got a reservation.

Roger Palms

Praise to You, God, for the reservation You have made
for me in Your eternal home.

Who, being in very nature God, did not consider
equality with God something to be grasped, but made himself
nothing, taking the very nature of a servant, being made
in human likeness.

(PHILIPPIANS 2 : 6 - 7)

Methought that in a solemn church I stood.
    Its marble acres, worn with knees and feet,
Lay spread from door to door, from street to street.
    Midway the form hung high upon the rood
Of Him who gave His life to be our good;
    Beyond, priests flitted, bowed, murmured meet
Among the candles shining still and sweet.
    Men came and went, and worshipped as they
could;
And still their dust a woman with her broom,
    Bowed to her work, kept sweeping to the door.
Then saw I slow through all the pillared gloom
    Across the church a silent figure come.
"Daughter," it said, "Thou sweepest well my floor!"
    "It is the Lord!" I cried, and saw no more.

George MacDonald

When I consider Your humility—Your choice to be a servant
for my sake—I bow before You in wonder and gratitude.

*Another angel, who had a golden censer, came and stood at
the altar. He was given much incense to offer, with the prayers
of all the saints, on the golden altar before the throne. The smoke
of the incense, together with the prayers of the saints,
went up before God from the angel's hand.*

(REVELATION 8:3-4)

What happens when God answers prayer? He pulls
back the curtain to the next act of our lives. And,
through His answer, lets us step into that next room of
our lives—open doors, spiritual maturity, accomplish-
ing His will on Planet Earth. One step nearer to the
Christlikeness He had planned for us before the foundation of the world.

And when we finally take that last step into God's
throne room, our prayers will be there—waiting for
us—with our Lord Himself.

Evelyn Christenson

*Thank You for each answered prayer, each step that
draws us closer to You and the scene that awaits us
when we finally see you in all Your glory!*

The Lord confides in those who fear him;
he makes his covenant known to them.

(PSALM 25:14)

Although it is the glory of God to conceal a matter, He reveals His secrets to those who revere and love Him. He takes them into His confidence.

How marvelous—God tells us His secrets. He becomes, as other translations put it, "intimate with those who fear Him." To the pure in heart are vouchsafed the secrets of the eternal God. Imagine, the God of the universe becoming personal and intimate with you and me. He tells us that He loves us and wants to live in our hearts forever. What marvelous condescension. What amazing grace!

Henry Gariepy

God of the universe, I marvel that You know who I am,
and want me to know you ... intimately.

But you will receive power when the Holy Spirit comes on you;
and you will be my witnesses in Jerusalem, and in all Judea
and Samaria, and to the ends of the earth.

(ACTS 1:8)

The missionary is one in whom the Holy Ghost has wrought this realization: "Ye are not your own." . . . Our Lord makes a disciple His own possession, He becomes responsible for him. "Ye shall be witnesses unto Me." The spirit that comes in is not that of *doing* anything for Jesus, but of being a perfect delight to Him. The secret of the missionary is—I am His, and He is carrying out His enterprises through me.

Oswald Chambers

I am Yours, Lord. Thank You that You send me out
with the promise of Your power.

We loved you so much that we were delighted to share with you not only the gospel of God but our lives as well, because you had become so dear to us.

(1 THESSALONIANS 2:8)

Anne Sullivan was born into a poor family, half blind. Then, at the Perkins Institute for the Blind, a brilliant operation restored Anne's sight. Thereafter she devoted herself to the care of the blind.

Meanwhile, down south a baby was born, a girl destined after early childhood never to see or speak or hear. This girl came under the care of Anne Sullivan, reluctantly at first. Yet with Anne's persistence, in two weeks, this girl had learned 30 words, spelling them by touching the hand of her teacher. This young woman, Helen Keller, grew to be known around the world. Teacher and pupil remained inseparable for 49 years.

Then Anne Sullivan's blindness returned. And now, the pupil taught the teacher how to overcome her lack of sight. She schooled her former teacher as devotedly as she had been schooled. Out of gratitude, Helen returned the grace to Anne.

John C. Maxwell

Thank You for family and friends—significant people who've shown me caring and love.

*But I have prayed for you, Simon, that your faith may not fail.
And when you have turned back, strengthen your brothers.*

(LUKE 22:32)

Have you hit the wall yet? You know what the wall is
. . . runners hit it in a marathon. They are going along
well, and suddenly they just run out of steam; they start
to stagger. And then it seems they get a second wind.
That happens to people spiritually too.

Jesus talked to Peter about that. He said, "I have
prayed for you that you will be able to keep on going."
He actually allowed for faith to hit the wall and a
second breath to come. Then, "Peter, once you get
back your wind, I have a job for you—to strengthen
other people."

You may be getting a second wind in order to reach
out and pull somebody else along, just as they may
have reached out and pulled you along. God gives us
new bursts of faith. We hit the wall and think we can't
go on. But we can go on, and because He is the
strength-giver, we can then offer strength to somebody
else.

Roger Palms

*Lord, I thank You for the people who have pulled me along
and for the joy of offering strength to someone else.*

*For this reason [Christ] had to be made like his brothers
in every way, in order that he might become a merciful and
faithful high priest in service to God, and that he might
make atonement for the sins of the people.*

(HEBREWS 2:17-18)

*O God, our Father, we remember at this time . . . how the eternal
Word became flesh and dwelt among us. . . . We thank you that
Jesus did a day's work like any working man, that he knew the
problem of living together in a family, that he knew the frustration
and irritation of serving the public, that he had to earn a living,
and to face all the wearing routine of everyday work and life and
living, and so clothed each common task with glory. . . .*

*We thank you that whatever happens to us, he has been there
before, and that, because he himself has gone through things, he is
able to help those who are going through them.*

William Barclay

So do not fear, for I am with you; do not be dismayed,
for I am your God. I will strengthen you and help you;
I will uphold you with my righteous right hand.

(ISAIAH 41:10)

The type of faith that conquers fear is the type in which the individual remains in constant fellowship with Jesus Christ. Since Christ is real, we can and we must experience fellowship with him and we must practice his presence in our lives. We must bind ourselves to Christ by a decisive act of commitment. Finally our faith must be big enough to encompass Christ's magnificent power and love. Only relational faith like this has the power to conquer our fears and calm our anxieties. That is why those two words of encouragement . . . "Fear not," are so frequently coupled with the promise from God, "for I am with you."

Charles D. Bass

You <u>are</u> with me, Jesus, just as You promised.
Why should I be anxious?

I have told you these things, so that in me you may
have peace. In this world you will have trouble. But take heart!
I have overcome the world. After Jesus said this, he looked toward
heaven and prayed:"Father, the time has come. Glorify your Son,
that your Son may glorify you.

(JOHN *16:33 – 17:1*)

In the secular world of the first century, glory was "the high opinion of others." In Scripture, however, "glory" is linked with the revelation of God's majesty. God's qualities are glorious in and of themselves. Jesus glorified God simply by doing God's will, and thus revealing what the Father is like.

How then do we glorify God? First, by recognizing His works and praising Him for the qualities His acts reveal. And second, by "bearing fruit." The stunning thought here is that as you and I live in intimate relationship with the Lord, He acts in and through us, thus revealing Himself to others. Like Jesus, we can glorify God by being channels through which the Lord reveals His beauty to mankind.

Larry Richards

I praise You, God, that You would use me
as a channel for Your love.

So then, just as you received Christ Jesus as Lord, continue to live in him, rooted and built up in him strengthened in the faith as you were taught, and overflowing with thankfulness.

(COLOSSIANS 2:6-7)

The secret of answered prayer is faith without doubt. And the secret of faith without doubt is praise, triumphant praise, continuous praise, praise that is a way of life.

Paul Billheimer

Is it a struggle for you to pray? Do your prayers seem lifeless to you? . . . Begin to give thanks for everything in your life for which you owe God thanks. And if you have any needs that you have asked God to supply in accordance with His promise, give thanks in advance that He will hear your prayers. . . . Such thanksgiving will draw down God's grace.

Basilea Schlink

Beautiful Savior,
    Lord of the Nations,
Son of God and Son of Man!
    Glory and honor,
    Praise, Adoration
Now and forevermore be thine!

Munster Gesangbuch, trans. Joseph Augustus Seiss

Sing to the Lord a new song; sing to the Lord, all the earth.
Sing to the Lord, praise his name; proclaim his salvation
day after day.

(PSALM 96:1-2)

Praise changes the way we view our lives. Had David focused only on his circumstances, he would have become hopelessly discouraged. But he didn't allow himself to remain fixed on the elements of his present situation. He focused on God—on His love and promises. He sang to the Lord "a new song" and received the encouragement his heart needed in order to continue doing what God wanted him to do at that moment.

Charles F. Stanley

Lord, rather than keeping my eyes on a problem situation,
thank You that I can focus them on You and Your promises.

*My mouth will tell of your righteousness, of your salvation
all day long, though I know not its measure. I will come and
proclaim your mighty acts, O Sovereign Lord; I will
proclaim your righteousness, yours alone.*

(PSALM 71:15-16)

O Lord, my Lord,
for my being, life, reason,
for nurture, protection, guidance,
for education, civil rights, religion,
for Thy gifts of grace, nature, fortune …
for Thy forbearance, long-suffering,
long long-suffering
toward me,
many seasons, many years, up to this time;
for all good things received, successes granted me,
good things done;
for the use of things present,
for Thy promise, and my hope
of the enjoyment of good things to come …
I bless Thee and will bless,
I give thanks to Thee and will give thanks,
all the days of my life.

Lancelot Andrewes

To them God has chosen to make known among the Gentiles
the glorious riches of this mystery, which is Christ in you,
the hope of glory.

(COLOSSIANS 1:27)

We remain faithful in hope. Ultimately—even if it be after seven years—our united appeal to the Father will intensify and accelerate the Kingdom's coming. The morning will dawn for our generation. With healing power, Christ will reveal Himself grandly in the midst of His Church before the eyes of the nations as the hope of glory. To that end we must struggle in prayer with all the energy God gives us.

David Bryant

The Christian can face the future with a holy optimism knowing that Jesus Christ is victor over all the powers of death, hell, and darkness. . . . To pray for the coming of the kingdom is to pray for the manifestation of deepening fulfillment of the victory of Jesus Christ in the life of the church and the world today as well as at the end of the age.

David Bloesch

You are the Victor, O Christ, and my hope is You, living in me.

The one who calls you is faithful and he will do it.

(*1 THESSALONIANS 5:24*)

It was the first Sunday night of April 1981, and the next morning I was to participate in my first Prison Fellowship national board meeting with Charles Colson. I knelt struggling in prayer in my motel room in Washington, D.C., telling the Lord how incapable I felt, how I was not smart enough to be on that board, how I was not able to do the job.

Finally I asked God for some Scripture so that I would have *His* words for me. I turned to 1 Thessalonians 5 where I was in my daily devotional reading. And there it was—verse 24.

The answer exploded within me. *I* don't have to do it. God will! I don't have to be all those things I know I can't be. *I* don't have to do those things I know I can't do. God will do them through me.

Evelyn Christenson

You comfort and encourage me, Lord, when You remind me that, when You give me an assignment, I don't need to be capable—You are.

He has taken me to the banquet hall,
and his banner over me is love.

(S O N G   O F   S O N G S   2 : 4)

I can still hear that chorus ("His banner over me is love") drawn from the lush love lyrics of the Song of Songs. So let's feast together with our Lord. Let's unfurl those banners that display just how much we love Him "because He first loved us."

This is the major scriptural image for our relationship with God—not a lecture hall, but a banquet hall; not a term paper due next Friday, but a dinner party this Sunday.

David New

Thank You, Lord, for inviting me to the party!

Let the little children come to me, and do not hinder them,
for the kingdom of God belongs to such as these.

(MARK 10:14)

Children eagerly crowded around Jesus. Then Jesus called to the adults huddled in the distance. "I tell you the truth, anyone who will not receive the kingdom of God like a little child will never enter it."

That's convicting! I want to change. I want to be a child again, but how can I, with a thousand adult-type responsibilities clinging to me? Still, if Jesus commands me to become like a child again, it must be possible.

The children were drawn to Jesus, and He welcomed them with open arms. Unafraid, they crawled in His lap, touched His face, stroked His beard. Their trust invited nearness. Their nearness enabled them to touch God and be blessed by Him.

Lorraine Pintus

I am grateful, Father, that You welcome me as I come to You,
childlike, in wide-eyed faith, wanting a touch from You.

And I will ask the Father, and he will give you another
Counselor to be with you forever—the Spirit of truth. The
world cannot accept him, because it neither sees him nor
knows him. But you know him, for he lives with you
and will be in you.

(JOHN *14:16-17*)

The Spirit is the pledge of the abiding presence of
Jesus, and of our fellowship with him. He imparts true
knowledge of his being and of his will. He teaches us
and reminds us of all that Christ said on earth. He
guides us into all truth so that we are not without
knowledge of Christ and the gifts which God has given
us in him. The gift which the Holy Spirit creates in us
is not uncertainty, but assurance and discernment.
Thus we are enabled to walk in the Spirit and to walk
in assurance.

Dietrich Bonhoeffer

Praise You, God, for sending Your Spirit to light my way.

Praise the Lord, all you nations; extol him, all you peoples.
For great is his love toward us, and the faithfulness of the Lord
endures forever. Praise the Lord.

(PSALM *117*)

Nothing is more powerful to engage our affection than to find that we are beloved. Expressions of kindness are always pleasing and acceptable unto us, but, to have the love of one who is altogether lovely, to know that the glorious Majesty of heaven hath any regard unto us, how must it astonish and delight us, how must it overcome our spirits and melt our hearts, and put our whole soul into a flame! Now, as the word of God is full of the expressions of his love toward man; so all his works do loudly proclaim it: he gave us our being, and, by preserving us in it, doth renew the donation every moment.

Henry Scougal

It is amazing, and it does delight my spirit, faithful God,
to read in Your Word that I am loved by You.

The Lord bless you and keep you ...
the Lord turn his face toward you and give you peace.

(NUMBERS 6:24,26)

In his book, *Peace of Mind*, Joshua Liebman tells of an experience he had as a young boy. He made a list of what he thought to be the best things in life and took them to a wise mentor. When he presented his list, including such treasures as health, beauty, riches, talents, friends, and faith, he expected to be praised for his discernment.

The wise old man reviewed the list, reached for a pencil, and drew a line through all the things Joshua had written down. Then the he said, "Young man, you may have all of these—health, beauty, riches, talents, friends, faith—but they will turn out to be enemies instead of friends unless you have the one thing you missed." Then he wrote on the paper: "The gift of an untroubled mind."

Amidst the turmoil, tragedies, and terrors of our world, Jesus Christ will give us the gift of an untroubled mind.

Henry Gariepy

Thank You, Jesus, for a mind untroubled and at peace with You.

Now may the Lord of peace himself give you peace at all times and in every way. The Lord be with all of you.

(2 THESSALONIANS 3:16)

The Old English root from which we get our word "worry" means "to strangle." If you have ever really worried, you know how it does strangle a person! In fact, worry has definite physical consequences: headaches, neck pains, ulcers, even back pains. Worry affects our thinking, our digestion, and even our coordination.

The antidote to worry is the secure mind. . . . When you have the secure mind, the peace of God guards you and the God of peace guides you! With that kind of protection—why worry?

Warren Wiersbe

Why worry, indeed, but You know I do, Lord.
Thank You for Your promise of peace which is mine
when I release the worry to You.

The Lord called Samuel a third time, and Samuel got up
and went to Eli and said, "Here I am; you called me." Then Eli
realized that the Lord was calling the boy. So Eli told Samuel,
"Go and lie down, and if he calls you, say, 'Speak, Lord, for your
servant is listening.' So Samuel went and lay down in his place.
The Lord came and stood there, calling as at the other time,
"Samuel! Samuel!"

(1 SAMUEL 3:8-10)

At this point in life I was simply complaining about
insomnia. . . . I would lie in bed and stew, angry because
I could not go back to sleep. When I told my psychologist friend this, he smiled, almost as if amused, and then
asked, "Has it ever occurred to you, Morton, that someone might be trying to get through to you? Don't you
remember how God called Samuel in the night?"

From then on I began to get up in the night and
write down my dreams and then try to listen. I soon
discovered that this was prime time for me—a time
when the telephone did not ring. . . . I found that I
could listen to God during this time and tell him about
my fears and anxieties, and what I had dreamed. After
about thirty minutes to an hour, with everything written down as best I could in a journal, I would go back
to bed and soon be asleep, my inner business in better
order.

Morton T. Kelsey

Thank You for using the quiet moments to call to me.

*All Scripture is God-breathed and is useful for teaching,
rebuking, correcting and training in righteousness.*

(2 TIMOTHY 3:16)

Books, many predict, will some day be out of style and,
like the typewriter, will yield to new technology.

But there is one book that must never become
outdated or obsolete. The Word of God is eternal.
Mankind will need its guidance and inspiration as long
as we inhabit this sin-stained planet. In his book *Helps
to Holiness*, Samuel Brengle called the Bible "God's
recipe book for making holy people, God's guide book
to show men and women the way to heaven, God's
doctor book to show people how to get rid of soul-
sickness."

Henry Gariepy

*I'm grateful, God, for the teaching, encouraging, enlightening,
even rebuking of Scripture.*

Give, and it will be given to you. A good measure, pressed down,
shaken together and running over, will be poured into your lap.
For with the measure you use, it will be measured to you.

(LUKE 6:38)

Lend your boat for a whole afternoon to Christ for His floating pulpit, and He will return it to you laden with fish. Place your upper room at His disposal for a single meal, and He will fill it and the whole house with the Holy Spirit of Pentecost. Place in His hands your barley loaves and fish, and He will not only satisfy your hunger, but add twelve baskets full of fragments.

We scratch the surface of the soil and insert our few little seeds, and within a few months the acreage is covered by a prolific harvest in which a hundredfold is given for every grain which we seemed to throw away.

F.B. Meyer

Gracious God, we cannot outgive You!

Do not be anxious about anything, but in everything, by prayer and petition, with thanksgiving, present your requests to God.

(PHILIPPIANS 4:6)

Among all the apostles none suffered so much as Paul; but none of them do we find so often giving thanks as he. Take his letter to the Philippians. Remember what he suffered at Philippi; how they laid many stripes upon him, and cast him into prison. Yet every chapter in that epistle speaks of rejoicing and giving thanks. There is that well-known passage: "Be careful for nothing, but in everything, by prayer and supplication, with thanksgiving, let your requests be made known unto God." (Phil. 4:6, KJV) As someone has said, there are here three precious ideas: "Careful for nothing; prayerful for everything; and thankful for anything." We always get more by being thankful for what God has done for us.

Dwight L. Moody

Again You remind me that You are ready to wipe away my worry, that You will answer. Thank You.

Ascribe to the Lord the glory due his name; worship the Lord in the splendor of his holiness.

(P S A L M 2 9 : 2)

Two days ago
You made the universe . . .
including man
praise God.
Yesterday
You lived among us . . .
taught healed and loved
died for our sins
rose from the dead
praise God.
Today You live in us . . .
praise God.
Tomorrow You'll return
to claim Your universe . . .
and every knee
in heaven and earth and under earth
shall bow
and every tongue confess
that You
are Lord
praise God.

Joseph Bayly

*I consider the present sufferings are not worth comparing
with the glory that will be revealed in us.*

(ROMANS 8:18)

I think it was the composer Franz Liszt who spoke about our lives being only a prelude, an overture, to the real symphony, the first note of which will be struck at our death. Think of it. We listen to the opening strains of music, and we anticipate the full orchestral beauty of the symphony.

Someday we will move past the beginning, past the prelude, past the overture, and when our friends are saying, "He is gone," we will have entered into a hall unlike any on earth for a symphony such as we have never heard before.

I am enjoying the overture now, but I am looking forward to the full symphony. Going home! There is so much to look forward to.

Roger Palms

*The overture is beautiful, Lord, but thank You
for the symphony that's coming!*

Grace and peace be yours in abundance through the knowledge
of God and of Jesus our Lord.

(2 PETER 1:2)

A mist was rising from the water and moving toward me. In a short while it enveloped the whole ship. I wrapped a blanket around me and snuggled down into a deck chair. Soon a fish leaped out of the water and a heron sailed majestically by. I felt like an eavesdropper on nature. It was pleasant and peaceful.

The mist enveloped me gently. It covered everything like a gossamer blanket . . . in the transitional world of early dawn it was a protective cover, screening, softening and beautifying everything.

I thought about God's grace and how all encompassing it is—like a universal and beneficent mist. No matter how great our sin or how isolated we may feel, God's grace creates for each of us a private pocket of forgiveness and reconciliation.

Leo Holland

Thank You for the protective cover of Your gentle grace.

Have Aaron your brother brought to you from among the Israelites along with his sons Nadab and Abihu, Eleazar and Ithamar, so they may serve me as priests. Make sacred garments for your brother Aaron, to give him dignity and honor.... Fashion a breastpiece for making decisions.... Then mount four rows of precious stones on it.

(EXODUS 28:1-2, 15A,17A)

Most of us will be unable to leave our children wealth or riches. But each of us does have an important gift we *can* give them—a sense of their worth, value, and specialness that reflects God's values, not the values of our society.

First, however, each of us needs to accept the gift God offers us in the symbolism of the jewels worn over the high priest's heart—the gift of realizing that *we* are special. Each stone bore the name of the forefather representing one of the tribes of Israel. God views each of us as an individual. Whatever our parents or our society may have implied, we have infinite worth and value to God. We are jewels. And He carries our names close to His heart.

Larry Richards

*How can I thank You, God, for knowing me—
for carrying my name close to Your heart!*

*For those God foreknew he also predestined to be conformed
to the likeness of his Son, that he might be the firstborn
among many brothers.*

(ROMANS 8:29)

God is in fact always passing into the everyday and
often colorless fabric of the life of each one of us. This
everyday experience may even be the sphere into
which he prefers to introduce his grace. The slightest
event in our lives and the least discernible movement
of his grace point to the passing of his justice and
mercy into our lives and to his desire to appeal to our
faithfulness and to draw us toward him.

He passes in this way among us in order to fashion us
into his form and likeness and to perfect us in his love.
Sometimes he does this slowly and silently, acting like
drops of water that take so many years to hollow out
the rock, and with so much discretion that we are
hardly aware of it. At other times, he acts so quickly
that he takes us by surprise.

Elisabeth-Paule Labat

*No matter how long it takes, nor in what manner, thank You
for Your patience in fashioning me into Your likeness.*

Forgive us our debts, as we also have forgiven our debtors.

(MATTHEW 6:12)

Ernest Hemingway, in his short story, "The Capital of the World," tells about a father and his teenage son who lived in Spain. Their relationship became strained, eventually shattered, and the son ran away from home. The father began a long journey in search of the lost and rebellious son, finally putting an ad in the Madrid newspaper as a last resort. His son's name was Paco, a very common name in Spain. The ad simply read: "Dear Paco, meet me in front of the Madrid newspaper office tomorrow at noon. All is forgiven. I love you." As Hemingway writes, the next day at noon in front of the newspaper office there were 800 "Pacos" all seeking forgiveness.

There are countless Pacos in the world who want more than anything else to be forgiven.

John C. Maxwell

I praise You for Your great, forgiving heart, Father God,
May it be reflected in the way I forgive others.

The Lord ... blesses the home of the righteous.

(P R O V E R B S 3 : 3 3)

In Proverbs the family holds the pivotal place in society. This book of Scripture portrays the family as the fundamental unit of the nation, as a cohesive bond of relationships. Husband, wife, parent, and children relationships receive constructive attention from this book of practical religion. What, after all, is more practical than family life? What is there nearer heaven than a family and home blessed by the presence and spirit of Christ in its midst?

Henry Gariepy

Thank You, Lord, that You want to be there
in the center of our homes—of our lives.

You are looking only on the surface of things.

(2 CORINTHIANS *10:7A*)

Pain forces you to look below the surface. But many of us never have the courage to choose to do that. Hence we waste much of our life in bitterness and complaint, always looking for something else, never realizing that perhaps God has already given us sufficient grace to discover all of what we are looking for in the midst of our circumstances.

St. Thomas Aquinas told of a man who heard about a very special ox and determined to have it for his own. He traveled all over the world. He spent his entire fortune. He gave his whole life to the search for this ox. At last, just moments before he died, he realized he had been riding it all the time.

Tim Hansel

Lord, You call me to see the grace You have
already provided for me. Thank You.

*Your righteousness reaches to the skies, O God, you who
have made me see troubles, many and bitter, you will
restore my life again; from the depths of the earth
you will again bring me up.*

(PSALM 71:19-20)

A friend of mine who manages a fast-food restaurant
had for months been in a stress-filled situation with his
assistant manager. The asssistant was constantly going
behind his back and complaining to the owner of the
store. The manager told me that one day he was so
overwhelmed by the pressure of the situation that he
cried out to God, "Why would You put me in a situation where I have to pray every five minutes just to
survive?" He realized he had answered his own question. God was using this stressful situation to draw that
manager closer to Himself and to demonstrate His
power in providing a miraculous solution to the problem. After a few months, the owner moved the assistant manager to another store. Stress can draw us
closer to God.

Robert Jeffress

*It's not easy to praise You for life's difficulties, God.
But right now I thank You for a particular stress and
that You can use it to draw me closer to You.*

*I have been crucified with Christ and I no longer live, but
Christ lives in me. The life I live in the body, I live by faith in
the Son of God, who loved me and gave himself for me.*

(G A L A T I A N S   2 : 2 0)

I am deeply convinced that when I allow God to enter
into my loneliness, when I allow him to let me know
that I am loved far more deeply than I can imagine,
only then can I give and receive real friendship. . . .
When I can say with Paul, "I no longer live, but Christ
lives in me," then I no longer need to depend on the
attention of others to have a sense of self. Because then
I realize that my most important identity is the identity
I have received as a grace of God and which has made
me a participant in the divine life of God himself.

Henri J.M. Nouwen

*What a relief, Lord. I don't need others to say, "You're okay."
You've already assured me of Your unconditional love.*

Do not store up for yourselves treasures on earth, where moth and rust destroy, and where thieves break in and steal.

(MATTHEW 6:19)

Anyone who has owned a piece of property for a length of time has seen its value fluctuate over the years. Anyone who has investments in stocks and bonds has seen both appreciation and depreciation.

We can plan all we want, but if we lay up for ourselves treasure upon earth, we have no guarantee that it is going to hold—which is exactly what Jesus meant. But He gives us an alternative: "store up for yourselves treasures in heaven."

When I bring someone along in the kingdom, that transaction is forever. When I yield myself to the living Christ and serve Him, the results are forever. When I worship Him, that praise doesn't end. These are investments that cannot be stolen and will not depreciate.

Roger Palms

Thank You for a "sure thing," Lord.
I choose the forever investment.

The man said, "This is now bone of my bones and flesh of my
flesh; she shall be called 'woman,' for she was taken out of man."
For this reason a man will leave his father and mother and be
united to his wife, and they will become one flesh.

(GENESIS 2:23-24)

Lord thank you
for this warm presence
here lying at my side
in holy dark.
Thank you
for beauty
present from the start
refined by sufferings
and joys
of forty years.
Thank you
for pureness, patience
faith and courage
love
that mounted
in crescendo
drums and cymbals
now muted quiet
flute and strings
and tiny bells.

Joseph Bayly

Thank You for the joy of human love.

But as for me, I will always have hope;
I will praise you more and more.

(PSALM 71:14)

Why does God expect us to live continuously with an attitude of thanksgiving? Because He knows how it will be of benefit to us. There is a surprising fringe benefit from a lifestyle of thankfulness. A medical doctor in Michigan said with great wisdom that the best way to handle stress is with an "attitude of gratitude." Why? Because there evidently are chemicals released in our bodies from such an attitude. The single best way to remove stress from life, the doctor had wisely concluded, is an *attitude of gratitude*.

Evelyn Christenson

You are my hope, Lord. I will praise You more and more.

*Praise the Lord. Praise the Name of the Lord; Praise him, you
servants of the Lord, you who minister in the house of the Lord,
in the courts of the house of our God. Praise the Lord, for the
Lord is good; sing praise to his name, for that is pleasant.*

(PSALM 135:1-3)

Thanksgiving, thanksgiving. All must be thanksgiving.
It took thirty-eight thousand Levites to give thanks
to God in David's day; every morning and every
evening the shifts changed. Four thousand were
needed just to carry the hacked carcasses of cattle, and
another four thousand were needed to sing about it.
The place reeked of blood, was soaked in blood. The
priests stood around gnawing and chewing and giving
thanks. They did not cross-stitch their gratitude on
samplers to frame and hang on the wall. They wrote
their thanks in blood on the doorposts every year.

Thanksgiving is not a task to be undertaken lightly.
It is not for dilettantes or aesthetes. One does not
dabble in praise for one's own amusement.

Virginia Stem Owens

Praise to You, Lord God, giver of life, lover of my soul.

Last night an angel of the God whose I am and whom I serve
stood beside me and said, "Do not be afraid, Paul. You must stand
trial before Caesar; and God has graciously given you the lives of
all who sail with you." So keep up your courage, men, for I have
faith in God that it will happen just as he told me.

(ACTS 27:23-25)

In a dense fog off the banks of Newfoundland, George
Muller . . . told the ship's captain, "I must be in Quebec
on Saturday afternoon." This was Wednesday. When
the captain said it was impossible, Muller replied, "If
your boat can't take me, God will find some other way.
I've never broken an engagement in fifty-seven years."

"I'd like to help," responded the captain, "but don't
you know how dense the fog is?"

"My eye is not on the fog, but on God. . . . Let's go
below and pray."

Down on his knees, Muller prayed a simple prayer.
"O Lord, if Thou wilt, remove this fog in five minutes."
Putting his hand on the captain's shoulder, Muller
restrained him from praying. "First, you don't believe
God will do it, and second, I believe He has already
done it. Open the door, Captain, and you'll find the
fog gone."

And so it was.

Leslie B. Flynn

My answers to prayer may not be so dramatic,
but thank You that they are just as real.

Take my yoke upon you and learn from me, for I am gentle
and humble in heart, and you will find rest for your souls.

(MATTHEW 11:29)

Rest, Rest, Rest in God's love. The only work you are
required now to do is to give your most intense attention to His still, small voice within.

Madame Jeanne Guyon

Through the Prayer of Rest God places His children in
the eye of the storm. When all around us is chaos and
confusion, deep within we know stability and serenity.
In the midst of intense personal struggle we are still
and relaxed. While a thousand frustrations seek to
distract us, we remain focused and attentive. This is
the fruit of the Prayer of Rest.

Richard Foster

Jesus, I am resting, resting
    In the joy of what Thou art.
I am finding out the greatness
    Of Thy loving heart.

Jean S. Pigott

May the God of peace, who through the blood of the eternal
covenant brought back from the dead our Lord Jesus, that great
Shepherd of the sheep, equip you with everything good for doing
his will, and may he work in us what is pleasing to him, through
Jesus Christ, to whom be glory for ever and ever. Amen.

(HEBREWS *13:21-21*)

For to be with Him brings joy and peace in the heart,
which is the greatest treasure in all life. It is the pearl
of great price, which is worth all the rest of the treasures of life together.

Believe me, now that I have reached old age, when
I say that this love of Christ in the heart is the truest
and best and greatest treasure that anyone can possibly
find in this life of ours. Jesus Himself said, "What shall
it profit a man, if he gain the whole world and lose his
own soul? and what shall a man give in exchange for
his soul?"

Charles F. Andrews

You are my treasure, Jesus. Your love is worth
more than anything else in life.

*Bring my sons from afar and my daughters from the ends of
the earth—everyone who is called by my name, whom
I created for my glory, whom I formed and made.*

(ISAIAH 43:6B-7)

Most of us spend time teaching our children that God
calls us, "His children." But God goes a step farther
than just saying we were created by Him. He declares
that He creates us for His glory. In other words, simply
by our obedience and love for God our lives declare
the glory of God. It is God's divine design that our
seemingly insignificant lives shout, "Hallelujah to the
King of Kings!"

So teach children that they have purpose. Teach
them that the God of all heaven and earth knows
them by name. He has a wonderful life filled with
excitement planned for them. Teach them that knowing God and following Him is more important than
anything else in the world!

David, Teresa, and Terri Ferguson
Paul and Vicky Warren

Hallelujah, King of Kings. May my life shout Your praise!

So if the Son sets you free, you will be free indeed.

(JOHN 8:36)

God does not, by the instant gift of His Spirit, make us always feel right, desire good, love purity, aspire after Him and His will. . . . He wants to make us in His own image, choosing the good, refusing the evil. How should He effect this if He were always moving us from within, as He does at divine intervals, toward the beauty of holiness? . . . For God made our individuality as well as, and a greater marvel than, our dependence; made our apartness from Himself, that freedom should bind us divinely dearer to Himself.

George MacDonald

Thank You that You made us to be free, Lord . . . not robots doing Your bidding, but free to serve You out of love.

Now the Lord God had planted a garden in the east, in Eden;
and there he put the man he had formed. And the Lord God
made all kinds of trees grow out of the ground—trees
that were pleasing to the eye and good for food.

(GENESIS 2:8-9A)

And then there is color. The Creator didn't have to
make a world in color. He could have wrapped it all in
battleship gray. Think of all the beautiful sunsets—one
every minute, all over the world. Picture the spongy
green of spring-fresh grass or the pink of a hyacinth or
crocus. In a recent news item about a middle-aged man
who gained his sight after a lifetime of blindness, the
awestruck man was quoted as saying, "I never imagined
that yellow could be so—*yellow*."

Joni Eareckson Tada

I praise You for bright yellows and intense blues and
brilliant reds. I praise You for shades of pink and soft brown
and jet black and purple and orange!

For I know that through your prayers and the help given
by the Spirit of Jesus Christ, what has happened to me will
turn out for my deliverance. I eagerly expect and hope that
I will in no way be ashamed, but will have sufficient courage
so that now as always Christ will be exalted in my body,
whether by life or by death.

(PHILIPPIANS 1:19-20)

I have come to the conclusion that I have actually been given a gift with my cancer—if I accept it as such. That gift is living in the today! Wringing out every drop of love and joy I can from the now. And then, being oh, so thankful, for things I took for granted before. It's a strange and painful, yet beautiful gift.

Because of this "gift" I am more tuned in to the spiritual activity around me. Lately I've been taking notice of other "plants" in my life. They always appear human, though sometimes I suspect they're angelic. (Maybe someday I'll get up my nerve to come right out and ask, "Are you an angel?") At any rate, these plants seem to be there at a time when I'm in need of a dose of courage or an attitude adjustment. I'm beginning to see a pattern in how God works with me.

Valerie Bell

To praise You for something like cancer, God, how can that be?
Yet, You show me every day that You can make
any experience of life a gift.

Finally, brothers, whatever is true, whatever is noble,
whatever is right, whatever is pure, whatever is lovely,
whatever is admirable—if anything is excellent
or praiseworthy—think about such things.

(PHILIPPIANS 4:8)

Victor Frankl was a Jewish psychiatrist who spent three grim years in a Nazi prison camp. He lived each hour with the realization that he might be among those who would be exterminated that day. Many who were interred with Frankl died from worrying about their death. Frankl chose not to do that. He developed a positive outlook which enabled him to peer through the broken slats in the wall of his cold hut and take pleasure in the beauty of a sunset. He developed a sense of humor so that he could laugh even in the midst of his pain. He found meaning in his suffering and he tried to help others find that meaning also.

Everything can be taken from man but one thing: the last of human freedoms—to choose one's attitude in any given set of circumstances, to choose one's way.

David Jeremiah

You make it possible, Father, for me to choose my attitude in
response to any circumstance. I can choose to notice the sunset.

No, in all these things we are more than conquerors
through him who loved us.

(ROMANS 8:37)

The surf that distresses the ordinary swimmer produces in the surf-rider the super-joy of going clean through it. Apply that to our own circumstances, these very things—tribulation, distress, persecution, produce in us the super-joy; they are not things to fight. We are more than conquerors through Him *in* all these things, not in spite of them, but in the midst of them. The saint never knows the joy of the Lord in spite of tribulation, but *because* of it.

Undaunted radiance is not built on anything passing, but on the love of God that nothing can alter. The experiences of life, terrible or monotonous, are impotent to touch the love of God, which is in Christ Jesus our Lord.

Oswald Chambers

Thank You that <u>nothing</u> can touch me without Your permission,
and <u>nothing</u> can keep me from Your love.

Take to heart all the words I have solemnly declared
to you this day.... They are not just idle words for you—
they are your life.

(DEUTERONOMY 32:46-47)

The Bible is God's love letter to me. I was sentenced to die, but God, through Jesus, courageously died in my place. One day we'll be together. Until then, I read and reread His letters. I pore over them, continually surprised to discover new things about the One I thought I knew so well. As I read, I sense Him beside me, pointing out things He wants me to know. His letters are my most precious possession. I weep that someone loves me so much.

One day I hope to know each page of the Bible as well as I know each page of *Goodnight Moon*. After I finish reading to my daughter, she always ask, "Can we read it again?" Wouldn't it be great if we felt that way about God's Word?

Lorraine Pintus

Thank You for the Bible, full of love notes from You to me.

Through Jesus, therefore, let us continually offer to God a
sacrifice of praise—the fruit of lips that confess his name.

(HEBREWS *13:15*)

Even if nothing else called for thankfulness, it would always be an ample cause for it that Jesus Christ loved us, and gave Himself for us. A farmer was once found kneeling at a soldier's grave near Nashville. Someone came to him and said: "Why do you pay so much attention to this grave? Was your son buried here?" "No," he said. "During the war my family were all sick, I knew not how to leave them. I was drafted. One of my neighbors came over and said: 'I will go for you; I have no family.' He went off. He was wounded at Chickamauga. He was carried to the hospital, and there died. And, sir, I have come a great many miles, that I might write over his grave these words, 'He died for me.'"

This the believer can always say of his blessed Savior, and in the fact may well rejoice.

Dwight L. Moody

Here, again, is my praise, Father, for sending Jesus
to be the sacrifice for my sin.

The heavens praise your wonders, O Lord....
O Lord God Almighty, who is like you?
You are mighty, O Lord, and your faithfulness
surrounds you.

(PSALM 89:5A, 8)

Praise to the Lord, the Almighty,
    the King of creation!
O my soul, praise Him,
    for He is thy health and salvation!
All ye who hear,
Now to His temple draw near;
Join me in glad adoration!

Praise to the Lord!
    O let all that is in me adore Him!
All that hath life and breath,
    come now with praises before Him.
Let the Amen
Sound from His people again:
Gladly for aye we adore Him.

Joachim Neander

Praise to You, Lord. You are my health and salvation.

Praise the Lord. Praise the Lord, O my soul. I will praise the Lord all my life; I will sing praise to my God as long as I live.

(PSALM 146:1-2)

On the afternoon of Thanksgiving Day itself . . . we were scheduled to sing within the Colorado women's penitentiary.

Holy, holy, holy. Who suckered us into this?

It wasn't even time, yet, for the concert to begin. . . . Yet the women were coming, and the practice piece drew a spattering of applause. "Soon and very soon, we are going to meet the king." Oh, the choir swung hard, and speedily against its beat . . . and the women laughed at our abandon, and behold: the song itself, it took us over! The nerves left us, and we too began to laugh as we sang . . . and the women took to clapping, some of them dancing with their faces to the floor, and their shoulders hunched, and they filled the place with their constant arrival, and somewhen—no one knew when—the practice turned into an honest concert, but there was no formality to it, because we were free, don't you see, free of the restraints of propriety, free of our fears, free to be truly, truly one with these women, free (Lord, what a discovery!) in prison.

Walter Wangerin, Jr.

In You there is freedom, Lord, even in prison.

*When the perishable has been clothed with the imperishable,
and the mortal with immortality, then the saying that is written
will come true: "Death has been swallowed up in victory."*

(1 CORINTHIANS 15:54)

While we don't know exactly how our bodies are going to be changed in that glorious day, we do know that the limitations and pain and suffering and death will be forever gone!

Our new bodies will be like the glorious body of our Lord Jesus Christ. Apart from the resurrection of Jesus Himself, there are only three resurrections recorded in the Gospels: the son of the widow of Nain, the daughter of Jairus, and Lazarus. All of these situations began in mourning until Jesus came; then that sorrow was turned into joy and gladness. Jesus said of Himself, "I am the resurrection and the life." Whenever the life of Jesus meets death, death is always defeated. When He comes again, death will be dealt its final blow.

David Jeremiah

*Who else could promise us victory over death,
but You, Lord Jesus Christ!*

God said to Moses, "I am who I am. This is what you are
to say to the Israelites: 'I AM has sent me to you.'"

(EXODUS 3:14)

I was regretting the past and fearing the future.
Sudenly my Lord was speaking to me.

"My name is I AM." He paused. I waited. He continued.

"When you live in the past, with its mistakes and
regrets, it is hard. I am not there. My name is not I
WAS.

"When you live in the future, with its problems and
fears, it is hard. I am not there. My name is not I WILL
BE.

"When you live in this moment, it is not hard. I am
here. My name is I AM."

Helen Mallicoat

Praise to You, God, the great I AM—
with me, here, in this moment!

Isn't this the carpenter? Isn't this Mary's son and
the brother of James, Joses, Judas and Simon?

(MARK 6:3)

How reassuring it is to know that He who now holds a
scepter in His hand once held a hammer and a saw. It
is a vivid portrait of the manhood of Jesus Christ.
Often His hands would be bruised and torn by the
grain. As He worked day after day, making the wood
obedient to His skill, His hands became as strong as a
vise. They became roughened and callused, the kind of
hands strong fishermen would look at and know that
they could follow Him with confidence and respect.
He knew the meaning of toil. He understands our
burdens, our weariness, our tasks.

Henry Gariepy

You've been there, Jesus. Thank You that You understand.

*Therefore, brothers, since we have confidence to enter the
Most Holy Place by the blood of Jesus, by a new and living
way opened for us through the curtain, that is, his body, and
since we have a great priest over the house of God, let us draw
near to God with a sincere heart in full assurance of faith, having
our hearts sprinkled to cleanse us from a guilty conscience and
having our bodies washed with pure water.*

(HEBREWS 10:19-22)

Arise, my soul, arise;
Shake off thy guilty fears;
The bleeding sacrifice
In my behalf appears:
Before the throne my surety stands,
Before the throne my surety stands,
My name is written on his hands.

My God is reconciled;
His pardoning voice I hear;
He owns me for his child;
I can no longer fear:
With confidence I now draw nigh,
With confidence I now draw nigh,
And, "Father, Abba, Father," cry. Amen.

Charles Wesley

*Abba, Father, because of Jesus I come to You
in grateful confidence.*

But because of his great love for us, God, who is rich in mercy, made us alive with Christ even when we were dead in transgressions—it is by grace you have been saved.

(EPHESIANS 2:4-5)

The God of Christmas is not a God who is simply the author of mathematical truths, or of the order of the elements; that is the view of heathens and Epicureans. He is not merely a God who exercises His providence over the life and fortunes of men, to bestow on those who worship Him a long and happy life. That was the portion of the Jews. But the God of Abraham, the God of Isaac, the God of Jacob, the God of Christians, is a God of love and of comfort, a God who fills the soul and heart of those whom He possesses, a God who makes them conscious of their inward wretchedness, and His infinite mercy, who unites Himself to their inmost soul, who fills it with humility and joy, with confidence and love, who renders them incapable of any other end than Himself.

Blaise Pascal

How can I thank You, Blessed God, for Your rich mercy? Not only have You saved me by Your grace, but You fill my soul with love and comfort and joy!

For where two or three come together in my name,
there am I with them.

(MATTHEW 18:20)

Nothing tends more to cement the hearts of Christians than praying together. Never do they love one another so well as when they witness the outpouring of each other's hearts in prayer.

Charles Finney

Jesus knew and spoke about the added power that comes when several are praying together. It is a most glorious experience of spiritual power, and of fellowship together.

Samuel M. Shoemaker

For the incomparable experience of uniting in prayer
with other believers, I thank You, God.

178

And this is my prayer: that your love may abound more and more in knowledge and depth of insight, so that you may be able to discern what is best and may be pure and blameless until the day of Christ, filled with the fruit of righteousness that comes through Jesus Christ—to the glory and praise of God.

(PHILIPPIANS *1:9-11*)

One of the greatest things I'm discovering is that I've often misread his signals. My fear of misguided sense of self-worth, my feelings of ungiftedness, or un-uniqueness, often block God's affirmation that comes from many places. During those moments I am denying his grace and personal investment in my humanness.

God has broken through to me often enough to help me begin to understand and experience the constancy of his grace. I'm now more able to celebrate my own feelings of self-worth and his investment in me—in each of us. I've come to accept myself as *a person of promise*. I now know that this ability to accept such healing affirmation is a gift of God!

Hal Edwards

You have made me a person of promise, Lord. You have gifted me with healing affirmations of my worth.

A cheerful heart is good medicine,
but a crushed spirit dries up the bones.

(PROVERBS *17:22*)

He was given a 1 in 500 chance of survival upon diagnosis of his disease. The prognosis: a degenerative spinal condition; time to finalize his will. That was in 1964. But instead, Norman Cousins turned to an unorthodox therapy. He took massive doses of laughter. He secured and watched Marx Brothers' movies and "Candid Camera" reruns and found that laughter gave him pain-free sleep. He continued laughing . . . his symptoms disappeared. He was cured.

Medical science is finding that laughter is good medicine. It is especially effective in fighting infections, stress, headaches, arthritis, gout, chronic allergies. "Bring in the clowns" may become a reality in medical units of the future!

Laughter is good for body and soul. God made us to laugh, as surely as He made us to breathe and to cry.

Henry Gariepy

My laughter rings out in joy and praise to You,
Creator of giggles.

Cast all your anxiety on him because he cares for you.

(1 PETER 5:7)

Every new dawn, before you awaken, life makes a delivery to your front door, rings the doorbell, and runs. Each package is cleverly wrapped. Put together they comprise a series of challenging opportunities brilliantly disguised as unsolvable problems. They are wrapped in paper with big print. One package reads: "Watch out—better worry about this!" Another: "Danger: this will bring fear!" And another: "Impossible, you'll never handle this one!"

When you hear the ring in the morning, try something new.

Have Jesus Christ answer the door for you.

Charles R. Swindoll

*Jesus, it's good news to me that You will "answer the door"—
that You will take my worries off my hands.*

Pray continually.

(*1* THESSALONIANS 5:17)

One morning in a church service an elderly man confessed that he wanted at last to place his trust in Jesus Christ as his Savior and Lord. Another elderly man in the congregation stood to his feet and in a voice quivering with emotion said, "For more than fifty years a group of men prayed for this friend. Those men have all gone home to heaven; I am the only one left to see God's answer to our prayers."

Those men had all witnessed to this man, had all prayed for him, had all had a part in giving a scriptural adomonition. The Holy Spirit had used them in their younger years as they cared for this one who now, at last, yielded his soul to God.

Roger Palms

Thank You, Lord, for times when You allow us to see answers to our prayers. But thank You, also, that when You don't, our prayers do not go unanswered.

*Give thanks to the Lord, call on his name; make known
among the nations what He has done, and proclaim
that his name is exalted.*

(ISAIAH 12:4)

Prayer, praise, and meditation on God's Word will lead
you to His will. Begin your journey of praise by making
a list of things that bring thoughts of thanksgiving. It
could be something as simple as the sunshine or a
friendship. You may be struggling with depression and
feel as though there is very little to be thankful for.
God knows your circumstances.

No matter how dark or black life appears, if you will
let Him, He will bring flashes of light and hope to your
world. If praise is difficult you can tell Him all about it.
Praise defuses depression.

Charles F. Stanley

*Lord, I thank You in advance for the flashes of light
You will bring to certain parts of my life today.*

*…always giving thanks to God the Father for everything,
in the name of our Lord Jesus Christ.*

(EPHESIANS 5:20)

When the humerus bone in Dave Dravecky's pitching arm snapped in two his baseball career was over, but his adversity had just begun. After many examinations, the doctors told him that his pitching arm would have to be amputated at the shoulder to guarantee that the cancer would not spread to other parts of his body. Dave was in the prime of his career, and under normal circumstances could have expected to play baseball for many more years. But now it was over.

Several weeks after his surgery, Dave Dravecky came back to Jack Murphy Stadium in San Diego. He was greeted with a long standing ovation. As on every other speaking assignment since he came out of the recovery room minus his left arm, he glorified God and gave praise to the name of Jesus.

Dravecky received over 700 invitations to speak during the next year. The apparent tragedy in his life had begun to take on a look of victory!

David Jeremiah

*You can take our greatest distresses and
turn them into victory parties, God.*

Then maidens will dance and be glad, young men
and old as well. I will turn their mourning into gladness;
I will give them comfort and joy instead of sorrow.

(JEREMIAH 31:13)

Recently a woman came to the house of prayer in Clearwater, Florida, where I am a staff member. She requested ministry for herself and family, giving a long history of problems with children, an alcoholic husband, her job, the neighbors—everything in her life was filled with gloom. I prayed with her but realized the task was monumental and she had to change her habit pattern of negativity.

On my advice, she purchased several tapes of praise music, promising to listen one hour each morning as she prepared for work. She returned several months later looking ten years younger and definitely happier. The problems at home hadn't changed but she discovered the recipe for happiness in the midst of pain. Thus with the psalmist she was able to say, "You have turned my mounring into dancing, you have stripped off my sackcloth and wrapped me in gladness; and now my heart, silent no longer, will play you music; Yahweh, my God, I will praise you for ever."

Barbara Shlemon

When I praise You, God, my mourning does turn
to dancing, my sorrow turns to joy!

But the Lord said to Ananias, "Go! This man is my
chosen instrument to carry my name before the Gentiles and
their kings and before the people of Israel."

(ACTS 9:15)

Three days after confronting Jesus on the Damascus
Road, Paul was told by Ananias that his ministry was
to bear the name of Jesus before Gentiles and kings.

For every gift He bestows, the Spirit has planned a
sphere of service. You are a gifted child of God. Since
you are also given an outlet for your gift, you are a
minister too. Thus, no child of God should have an
inferiority complex. Rather, awareness that you are a
gifted child with an area of ministry should meet your
psychological need to feel wanted and to possess a
sense of worth. No false humility should make you
moan, "I'm a nobody," and lead you to bury your gifts
and hear the ultimate verdict: "slothful servant."

Leslie B. Flynn

You have gifted me for ministry as Your own child,
Heavenly Father, and I thank You that I can be useful to You.

As a father has compassion on his children,
so the Lord has compassion on those who fear him.

(PSALM *103:13*)

I think a lot of what I believe about God, my Heavenly Father, has come from my relationship with my dad. I remember when I was a young girl, Dad would always put me to bed and pray with me before I went to sleep. That taught me stuff about God at a real basic level. Looking back now as a twenty-one-year-old adult, it means more to me now than it did then. It helped me realize what was the most important thing in life—to be close to God. . . . I see God as security now—someone I can trust and believe in, someone who won't let me down no matter what I do. I know that a big part of that comes from what my own dad showed me.

"Janna"

Thank You for fathers and mothers who model Your
Father/Mother love for us so we can see You better.

After Job had prayed for his friends, the Lord made him
prosperous again and gave him twice as much as he had before.

(J O B 4 2 : 1 0)

We must not misinterpret the final chapter of Job and conclude that every trial will end with all problems solved, all hard feelings forgiven, and everybody "living happily ever after." It just doesn't happen that way! Scripture assures us that, no matter what happens to us, *God always writes the last chapter.* Therefore, we don't have to be afraid. We can trust God to do what is right, no matter how painful our situation might be.

But Job's greatest blessing was not the regaining of his health and wealth or the rebuilding of his family and circle of friends. His greatest blessing was *knowing God better and understanding His working in a deeper way.*

Warren Wiersbe

As I look back, Lord, I see that I don't have to be afraid.
You have been there in every situation, no matter
how painful. Thank You.

*Your kingdom come, Your will be done
on earth as it is in heaven.*

(MATTHEW 6:10)

Christ's kingdom, or kingship, is wherever He is recognized as King, His will is obeyed, and subjects reap the benefit of His rule.

Heaven is that way. All subjects there bow before Christ as King. In heaven all are obedient to His will and reap great benefits. So heaven is the kingdom, or kingship, of Christ.

But the kingdom is here as well. When we bow to Christ as Lord and obey His will, we are the ones who benefit as we live under His gracious kingship. Kingdom people believe in restoration—release from oppression in Egypt and even worse settings. It is the King's ultimate dream for the world that we cherish.

David Mains

*I worship You, my King, and wait for You
to restore Your kingdom.*

*The Lord delights in the way of the man whose steps
he has made firm; though he stumble, he will not fall,
for the Lord upholds him with his hand.*

(PSALM 37:23-24)

A group of tourists in the highlands of Scotland saw a
rare plant on the side of a cliff. There was no way to
approach it. Upon seeing a boy helping his father keep
the sheep in a field, they asked him to allow them to
lower him over the cliff on a rope. The boy hesitated.
They promised him a liberal reward. Finally he said he
would do it under one condition. "I will do it," he said,
"if my father holds the rope." We too can face with
confidence the difficult and dangerous testings of life if
we know we are in the hands of our Father.

Henry Gariepy

*Thank You for holding my hand, Father,
for with You I can face anything.*

Every good and perfect gift is from above, coming down from the Father of the heavenly lights, who does not change like shifting shadows.

(JAMES 1:17)

Every good thing comes from the Father. Every single one. And more than that, those good things are *gifts*. Gifts to be received with heartfelt gratitude. As David wrote, "How precious to me are your thoughts, O God! How vast is the sum of them! Were I to count them, they would outnumber the grains of sand." (Ps. 139:17-18)

Even though our own pain might scream for our undivided attention, God wants us to come to Him with a heart full of thankfulness for all the good things in this life. Everything from the joy of a Christ-centered friendship to the first lick of a Baskin-Robbins pistachio ice cream cone.

Every good gift comes from the same Giver.

Joni Eareckson Tada

Father God, when I start counting Your gifts—just those You've given me today—I'm overwhelmed with Your care for me.

For everyone who has will be given more, and he will have
an abundance. Whoever does not have, even what he has
will be taken from him.

(MATTHEW 25:29)

God sets us free to be our real selves, that is, to create, to dream, to love, to care, to listen, to be a friend to our fellows. He sets us free from the early training that has inhibited or warped us. He gives us the power to break through self-consciousness and the fear of rejection. We are free to love and care with an imaginative awareness of the needs of others.

We are set free also to use the talents God has given us. In the parable of the talents, the man who had only one was afraid, and buried his capacities (Matt. 25:25). God sets us free from this kind of fear, free to use our inner potential with ever-increasing confidence. We are free indeed when we are free to fulfill the blueprint that God has drawn for our lives.

Lionel A. Whiston

Thank You that You want to free me to be my true self, God—
to realize the potential of the gifts You have given me.

By faith Abraham, even though he was past age—and Sarah
herself was barren—was enabled to become a father because
he considered him faithful who had made the promise.

(HEBREWS *11:11*)

If you are facing the unpredictable right now in your
life, I suggest you look for God's gift to you in it. The
uninterrupted routine of work, eat, sleep, play—
however pleasant—is not enough for any of us. It is
those new, unexpected challenges that force us to
depend upon the resources of God and to find the
inner strength he gives.

Bruce Larson

Lord, thank You that life with You is not dull. And thank You
that with the challenges you bring the resources to meet them.

Therefore, since we have been justified through faith, we have peace with God through our Lord Jesus Christ, through whom we have gained access by faith into this grace in which we now stand. And we rejoice in the hope of the glory of God.

(ROMANS 5:1-2)

On May 24, 1738, a discouraged missionary went "very unwillingly" to a religious meeting in London. There a miracle took place. "About a quarter before nine," he wrote in his journal, "I felt my heart strangely warmed. I felt I did trust in Christ, Christ alone, for salvation; and an assurance was given me that He had taken away my sins, even mine, and saved me from the law of sin and death."

That missionary was John Wesley. The message he heard that evening was the preface to Martin Luther's commentary on Romans. Paul's Epistle to the Romans is still transforming people's lives, just the way it transformed Martin Luther and John Wesley.

Warren Wiersbe

Praise You, God, that we have access to the transforming message of Scripture.

Sing to God, O kingdoms of the earth, sing praise to the Lord, to him who rides the ancient skies above, who thunders with mighty voice. Proclaim the power of God, whose majesty is over Israel, whose power is in the skies. You are awesome, O God, in your sanctuary; the God of Israel gives power and strength to his people. Praise be to God!

(PSALM 68:32-35)

If the words *praise* and *worship* share anything in common, it is this: When we praise and worship God we are doing the most unselfish thing we could possibly do. True praise and worship permit no self-centeredness. We must step outside of our own complaints, irritations, and desires, focusing instead on the greatness of God.

Joni Eareckson Tada

All hail, Redeemer, hail!
For Thou hast died for me:
Thy praise shall never, never fail
Throughout eternity!

Matthew Bridges/Godfrey Thring

Where, O death, is your victory?
Where, O death, is your sting?

(*1* CORINTHIANS *15:55*)

On the morning of Dwight L. Moody's death his son, who was standing by the bedside, heard him exclaim, "Earth is receding; heaven is opening; God is calling." "You are dreaming, Father," the son said. Moody answered, "No, Will, this is no dream. I have been within the gates. I have seen the children's faces."

For a while it seemed as if Moody was reviving, but he began to slip away again. He said, "Is this death? This is not bad; there is no valley. This is bliss. This is glorious." By this time, his daughter was present, and she began to pray for his recovery. He said, "No, no, Emma, don't pray for that. God is calling. This is my coronation day. I have been looking forward to it."

At the funeral the family and friends joined in a joyful service. They sang hymns. They heard the words proclaimed, "O death, where is thy sting? O grave, where is thy victory? . . . Thanks be to God, who giveth us the victory through our Lord Jesus Christ."

David Jeremiah

Thank You, Lord, for removing the reason to fear death.

If you really knew me, you would know my Father as well.
From now on, you do know him and have seen him.

(JOHN 14:7)

The moment you press your ear against [Jesus'] heart, you instantly hear Abba's footsteps in the distance. I do not know how this happens. It just does. It is a simple movement from intellectual cognition to experiential awareness that Jesus and the Father are one in the Holy Spirit, the bond of infinite tenderness between Them. Without reflection or premeditation the cry, "Abba, I belong to You," rises spontaneously from the heart. The awareness of being sons and daughters in the Son dawns deep in our souls, and Jesus' unique passion for the Father catches fire within us. In the Abba experience we prodigals, no matter how bedraggled, beat-up, or burnt out, are overcome by a Paternal fondness of such depth and tenderness that it beggars speech. As our hearts beat in rhythm with the Rabbi's heart, we come to experience a graciousness, a kindness, a compassionate caring that surpasses our understanding.

Brennan Manning

Abba, I belong to You. Thank You.

Then the cloud covered the Tent of Meeting, and the glory
of the Lord filled the tabernacle. Moses could not enter the
Tent of Meeting because the cloud had settled upon it,
and the glory of the Lord filled the tabernacle.

(EXODUS 40:34-35)

The Tabernacle erected in the camp [of the Israelites] was tangible evidence that God, their delivering God, had come to dwell with His people. . . The great, good news for God's people today is that He is in our midst. He is not in a cloud, or a pillar of fire. He is not in a Tabernacle, or a temple. The Holy Spirit of our delivering God is in the hearts of His faithful people. We may turn to other idols temporarily, but His love and forgiveness are certain. We may feel abandoned, cut off by illness, loss, misfortune, but help is always on the way. We are promised not just deliverance, but the love and presence of the Deliverer.

Bruce Larson

Delivering God, I praise You for Your love and presence here,
now, always accessible.

*But now a righteousness from God, apart from law, has
been made known, to which the Law and the Prophets testify.
This righteousness from God comes through faith in Jesus Christ
to all who believe. There is no difference, for all have sinned and
fall short of the glory of God, and are justified freely by his grace
through the redemption that came by Christ Jesus.*

(ROMANS 3:21-24)

What a wonderful breadth of divine charity! He who is
altogether righteous will accept from us even the thirst
for righteousness. He will not reserve his blessing until
I become actually pure; he will bless my very effort
after purity. He will accept the mere desire for him; the
mere wish of my heart to be like him; the mere throb
of my pulse to be near him. Tho I have not reached
him, if only I see in him a beauty that I long for, he will
count it unto me for righteousness.

George Matheson

*Great God, how grateful I am that You have not waited to
hold out to me Your grace until I became actually pure.
Thank You for Your unconditional love.*

One thing I do: Forgetting what is behind and straining toward what is ahead, I press on toward the goal to win the prize for which God has called me heavenward in Christ Jesus.

(PHILIPPIANS 3:13B-14)

Strong finishers are people committed to personal reformation. That is, these people are eager to maintain a vibrant, active, authentic, spiritual life both present and future. Truthfully, experiencing personal reformation or getting back to your spiritual future is a never-ending journey, a process that's ongoing.

Change, growth, deepening, and spiritual risk-taking are all normative to a vital Christian life. "The best is still ahead" is a valid motto for the believer who holds to this dynamic, spiritually healthy mind-set. Such a person continues to dare to dream, to make God's dreams his or her own. Said differently, there's no retirement plan in the life of faith!

Steve and Valerie Bell

Thank You that the best is still ahead. Thank You that You encourage me to dream.

So do not worry, saying, "What shall we eat?" or "What shall
we drink?" or "What shall we wear?" For the pagans run after
all these things, and your heavenly Father knows that you need
them. But seek first his kingdom and his righteousness,
and all these things will be given to you as well.

(M A T T H E W   6 : 3 1 - 3 3)

I called from the office and asked my wife, Karen,
"Where are you money-wise?" I needed to head home
and pack. We were using some frequent flyer award
tickets to take a couple of well-deserved days away. I
had very little cash in the bank, although I figured we
could use a credit card if need be. But maybe Karen
had money.

Her anwer was, "My bank account is as low as
yours!"

"Just wondered," I responded. "See you soon."

In the next few moments an old friend stopped by
the office and said, "Heard you and Karen were leaving
for a few days. Knowing how you guys live, I thought
you might need some cash. It's a gift; don't give it back.
Have a good time. The Lord go with you."

I praise the Lord for friends and *also* for unexpected
evidences like this of God's care.

David Mains

Thank You, Lord, for the times You've used friends
to communicate Your care.

There was given me a thorn in my flesh, a messenger
of Satan, to torment me. Three times I pleaded with the
Lord to take it away from me.

(2 C O R I N T H I A N S   12:7B-8A)

Joni Eareckson Tada testifies: "My paralysis has drawn
me close to God and given a spiritual healing which I
wouldn't trade for a hundred active years on my feet."
Fulton Sheen records in his autobiography: "The
greatest gift of all may have been His summons to the
cross, where I found His continuing self-disclosure."
The turning point in the life of Martin Luther came
when his friend, Alexis, struck by lightning, fell dead
at his feet.

Sickness, adversity, death, a crossroad—can become
spiritual landmarks where we may hear and heed the
call of God. C.S. Lewis reminds us that "God whispers
to us in our pleasures, but shouts in our pains."

Henry Gariepy

Though I don't welcome pain and trouble,
You do get my attention that way, Lord.

There remains then a Sabbath-rest for the people of God;
for anyone who enters God's rest also rests from his own work,
just as God did from his. Let us, therefore, make every effort
to enter that rest.

(H E B R E W S 4 : 9 - 1 1 A)

It is God's own rest. It is the realm in which the future is assured, for every contingency has been planned for. We enter that rest by responding to God's voice with faith and obedience. He who knows the future can and will guide us safely through our today. The voice of Him who has solved every problem will lead us to His solutions. The voice of the One who knows every need will guide us to the place where our needs will be met. Our struggle is not to find our way into tomorrow, but to submit to His will, so that He can guide us to where we must be.

Larry Richards

Father, thank You that I can relinquish any burden
I'm clinging to and sink into Your rest.

Jesus looked at them and said, "With man this is impossible, but now with God; all things are possible with God."

A man who owns an airport once told me that when the pressures of life got too great and he found himself reduced to fear, there was always something that greatly helped. He took one of the planes and spent an hour flying. The higher he flew, the smaller his problems became. In the stillness and aloneness and at the great height he felt close to God, and thought, "How small my problems must seem to my Heavenly Father. Truly all things are possible with Him, nothing shall be impossible."

When we saturate our minds in the majestic glory and purposes of God, and when the things of earth are considered from this perspective, impossibilities are no longer impossibiliites. We can face the problems of life with a courageous spirit and a serene mind, free of concern and fear.

Norman Elliott

Thank You for helping me see things from Your perspective, Heavenly Father, that nothing is impossible with You.

I will give you a new heart and put a new spirit in you;
I will remove from you your heart of stone and give you
a heart of flesh.

(EZEKIEL *3 6 : 2 6*)

Is it springtime right now in your season of life? Perhaps you're awakening from spiritual hibernation, crawling slowly out of a dark cave of disillusionment and discouragement. Don't be afraid to try again. That's the sun out there! It invites you to try out its splendor . . . to believe anew. To realize that the same Lord who renews the trees with buds and blossoms, who renews the grass with green in place of brown, is ready to renew your life with hope and courage.

Charles R. Swindoll

Oh Lord, I rejoice in Your promise that spring will come.

...in order that I may boast on the day of Christ that I did not run or labor for nothing.

(PHILIPPIANS 2:16B)

You may not see all your victories. You may not know all that your faithfulness means to the larger body of believers. You may not know how your ministry is affecting the kingdom work. But if you are holding fast to the Word of Life, then what you do is not a waste of time and your life has had meaning. You are not running or toiling in vain. The faithful never do run in vain. What they do always counts.

Roger Palms

To know that my running is not in vain gives me courage to keep going, Lord.

Enter his gates with thanksgiving and his courts with praise;
give thanks to him and praise his name.

(PSALM 100:4)

More than 25 years ago, I made it my life's aim to pursue and to be pursued by God. Thankfulness is where that journey begins. . . . This practice of giving thanks has led me to face the degeneration of one of my eyes with an entirely different attitude than I would have had several years ago. There's nothing the doctors can do to stop it, but I think it actually bothers others more than me. Why?

I trust God. Whatever happens, I know He is going to use it, somehow, for His purposes. Fretting about it won't heal my eye. But thanking God for all that He has done, is doing, and will do, will certainly heal my spirit.

Gary Thomas

Lord, thank You for turning our problems
into springboards for praise.

*Therefore, since we are surrounded by such a great
cloud of witnesses, let us throw off everything that hinders
and the sin that so easily entangles, and let us run with
perseverance the race marked out for us.*

(HEBREWS *12:1*)

*Blessed, and praised, and celebrated,
and magnified, and exalted, and glorified,
and hallowed,
be Thy Name, O Lord,
its record, and its memory,
and every memorial of it;
for the all-honorable senate of the Patriarchs,
the ever-venerable band of the Prophets,
The all-glorious college of the Apostles,
the Evangelists,
the all-illustrious army of the Martyrs....
Glory to Thee, O Lord, glory to Thee,
glory to Thee who didst glorify them,
among whom we too glorify Thee.*

Lancelot Andrewes

Blessed are those who have learned to acclaim you,
who walk in the light of your presence, O Lord.

(PSALM 89:15)

If we give thanks only when we have scored the goal, received a raise, received a healthy grandchild, then we are in danger of turning God into a Santa Claus divinity. Our gratitude becomes conditional. We get, then give thanks.

God is not the one who comes occasionally, bearing gifts, Rather, God is the One who is with us at all times. "The Lord is near at hand," says Paul. It is God's very Presence, not merely God's blessings, for which we give thanks. "God is here! Rejoice! Give thanks!" You have God with you every day, in all things. To be awake to the presence of God brings rejoicing and gratitude . . . and our sense of gratitude changes, from being thankful for, to simply being thankful.

Dan Chambers

Far above all Your kindnesses to me—food, clothing,
sheleter, and so much besides—I thank You for Your presence:
constant, close as breath,* comforting.

For we walk by faith, not by sight.

(2 CORINTHIANS 5:7)

In Bristol, England, George Muller cared for 10,000 orphans over a period of sixty years. He received enough to build five large homes to house 2,000 orphans, and daily food for them, all by faith and prayer.

One morning when not a speck of food or milk was at hand to feed the hundreds of hungry orphans breakfast, Mr. Muller prayed, "Father, we thank Thee for the food Thou art going to give us."

Came a knock at the door. A baker stood there. "I was awakened at 2 A.M. and felt I should bake some bread for you."

A few minutes later came another knock. A milkman said, "My milk wagon just broke down in front of your place. I must get rid of these cans of milk. Can you use them?" Muller testified that thousands of times they were without food for another meal and without funds, but not once did God fail to provide food.

Leslie B. Flynn

Thank You for Your faithfulness to trusting saints like Muller, and the encouragement to step out in faith as they did.

God is love. Whoever lives in love lives in God,
and God in him.

(1 JOHN 4:16B)

Through the simplicity of children God reminds us of the important things in life.

One evening at dinner my four-year-old son was so overtaken by the day that he was singing a little home-made song: "I was walking along and saw a dog—and he said bow wow. And the cat said meow, and the cow said moo. And I was walking along and I saw some flowers . . ."

There was a rather long pause, so I asked innocently, "And what did they say?"

"And they said, 'Jesus loves me, this I know, for the Bible tells me so.'"

When you are four, God is everywhere, and He is love.

Tim Hansel

Praise to You, God, for four-year-old trust . . .
the kind You said should be our model.

Sing to the Lord, all the earth; proclaim his salvation
day after day. Declare his glory among the nations,
his marvelous deeds among all peoples.

(*1* CHRONICLES *16:23-24*)

God's bigger dreams quickly come into sharper focus
when we're reminded of His involvement in our lives.
When this happens, though, it's also true that the
enemy engages us in fiercer combat.

Even so, I say, "Good for you!" to those who have
trained themselves to recognize God in the every day.
These are the men and women who find it easiest to
sustain their believe in God's long-range dreams.
That's because they see daily evidence that the Lord
hasn't forsaken them.

David Mains

Lord, how exciting to watch for You in the circumstances
of each day and find You there!

*The seventh angel sounded his trumpet, and there were
loud voices in heaven, which said: "The kingdom of the world
has become the kingdom of our Lord and of his Christ,
and he will reign for ever and ever."*

(REVELATION 11:15)

We live in a day when God has set aside the open
exercise of His mighty power. He works now through
providence, so subtly that the lost laugh at the notion
of divine sovereignty, and pass all things off as chance
or happenstance. One day God will openly take up His
mighty power, and then His rule will be unmistakable.
And that day is coming, soon.

Until then, we must remember that when things
look darkest on the earth, the songs of heaven are the
most triumphant. You and I, limited to our physical
eyes, may not see what is so clear in heaven. But we
can still rise up, and shout it out with the angels: "God
reigns!"

Larry Richards

*I praise You, God, that even though now Your reign is subtle
and hidden to many, You do reign!*

For by him all things were created: things in heaven and on earth, visible and invisible, whether thrones or powers or rulers or authorities; all things were created by him and for him.

(COLOSSIANS 1:16)

Before Jesus ever came to earth, His hands tumbled solar systems and galaxies into space. He set the stars on their courses. He kindled the fires of the sun. He scooped out the giant beds of our mighty oceans.

He created not only the macroscopic with its fiery planets and its unimaginable reaches of intergalactic space, but He created the microscopic as well. He polished the eye of every tiny insect, painted the bell of the lily, and crafted the exquisite geometry of the snowflake. He is the One who has made "all things bright and beautiful, all things great and small."

Henry Gariepy

Glory and praise to You, Jesus, Creator God, for the beautiful world You have made for us!

Be joyful in hope, patient in affliction, faithful in prayer.

(ROMANS *12:12*)

Thousands of Christians have learned the secret of contentment and joy in trial. Some of the happiest Christians I have met have been life-long sufferers. They have had every reason to sigh and complain, being denied so many privileges and pleasures that they see others enjoy, yet they have found greater cause for gratitude and joy than many who are prosperous, vigorous and strong. In all ages Christians have found it possible to maintain the spirit of joy in the hour of trial. In circumstances that would have felled most men, they have so completely risen above them that they actually have used the circumstances to serve and glorify Christ.

Billy Graham

To our places of pain, You come with gifts of joy.

*I am not ashamed of the gospel, because it is the power of God
for the salvation of everyone who believes: first for the Jew, then
for the Gentile. For in the gospel a righteousness from God is
revealed, a righteousness that is by faith from first to last,
just as it is written: "The righteous will live by faith."*

(ROMANS *1:16-17*)

The one Scripture above all others that brought
Luther out of mere religion into the joy of salvation by
grace, through faith, was this passage in Romans. The
Protestant Reformation and the Wesleyan Revival
were both the fruit of this wonderful letter.

Imagine! You and I can read and study the same
inspired letter that brought life and power to Luther
and Wesley! And the same Holy Spirit who taught
them can teach us! You and I can experience revival in
our hearts, homes, and churches if the message of this
letter grips us as it has gripped men of faith in centuries
past.

Warren Wiersbe

*We are so blessed, Father, to have the same powerful Word
that impacted great hearts of past ages.*

By the meekness and gentleness of Christ, I appeal to you …

(2 CORINTHIANS 10:1A)

Thank You
Lord Christ
for treating every other person
as an end
not a means
including me.
Thank You
that you never climbed
on other person's shoulders
never used a man or woman
boy or girl
as if he were a thing.
Thank You
for refusing to invade
the freedom
You have given us.
Thank You for refusing
to manipulate us
pressure us
maneuver us into a corner.
Thank You for treating us
as if we shared Your image.

Joeseph Bayly

COUNT Your BLESSINGS

For he himself is our peace, who has made the two one and has destroyed the barrier, the dividing wall of hostility.

(EPHESIANS 2:14)

When the wall came down between East and West Berlin, there was a spontaneous national holiday. Well, there's another wall that has come down. Think of it. The wall separating us from God has been torn down. He broke down the wall and said, "Come on through." Through Jesus Christ, He opened the way.

When people recognize what God has done in Christ Jesus, tearing down the dividing wall of hostility, there is a spontaneous rejoicing as well. We praise, we worship, we say over and over again, "Thank You, God."

Roger Palms

Thank You, God, that through Christ Jesus You have broken down the wall that separated me from You.

*However, the Lord your God would not listen to Balaam
but turned the curse into a blessing for you, because the
Lord your God loves you.*

(DEUTERONOMY 23:5)

While it's very difficult
for mankind to understand
God's intentions and His purpose
and the workings of His hand,
If we observe the miracles
that happen every day,
We cannot help but be convinced
that in His wondrous way
God makes what seemed unbearable
and painful and distressing
Easily acceptable
when we view it as a blessing.

Helen Steiner Rice

*It's those everyday miracles—seeing Your hand in both the
large and small moments—that keep us going, Lord.*

*He will judge between many peoples and will settle
disputes for strong nations far and wide. They will beat
their swords into plowshares and their spears into pruning
hooks. Nation will not take up sword against nation,
nor will they train for war anymore.*

(MICAH 4:3)

In the 1949, during the Cultural Revolution in China,
The Salvation Army was disbanded and Major Hung
Shun Yin with others was forced to work in the labor
camps for over thirty years. But all through that time
he kept alive his love of the Lord.

When in 1981 he came to the U.S.A. for the first
time, there were three things he wanted to see: the
national headquarters of The Salvation Army, the
Statue of Liberty, and the sculpture in front of the
U.N. that has this inscription from Micah 4:3.

Let us, from this ancient text, take hope for the
future. God's loving purpose for man will not be
aborted. Wars and violence and sin will ultimately be
ended and God's peace shall reign.

Henry Gariepy

Praise to You, Great God my Savior. Your peace shall reign.

The Lord appeared to us in the past, saying:
"I have loved you with an everlasting love;
I have drawn you with loving-kindness."

(JEREMIAH 31:3)

For twenty-three years I worked to earn people's love. Then God introduced me to a new kind of love. Unconditional love. Not the kind of love that says, "I love you if . . ." or "I love you when . . ." but the kind of love that says, "I love you." Period.

I tested God's love for me. I did bad things, things I knew disappointed Him. Still He assured me, "I love you." Eventually, my resistance to His love broke, and I was set free. Free from my performance-oriented nature . . . free to love and be loved in a deeper way than I had ever known before.

Lorraine Pintus

Lord, Your unconditional love sets me free.

This is how you should pray: "Our Father in heaven ..."

(MATTHEW 6:9A)

"Teach us to pray."

And he did. "Do it this way," he told them.

"When you pray say, 'Our Father,'" Dear Abba. The first tentative and informal sound made at the baby's first taste of wheat.

Father. KINFOLKS!

Not "Our God." Gods aren't kin to folks. "Our Father." No doubt they had heard God referred to as Father before, but not very often. Most often the image they heard the rabbis use was of King. Or Lord. The idea of sonship, of actual kinship had not been developed. Fathers are kinfolks! God is God and a human is a human. God has claims and designs on us but we have no claims and designs on God. God is God. But kinfolks have claims and designs on each other. Kinfolks ask each other for things: Give us some bread, something to eat. Don't hold things against us. Forgive us. Excuse and understand. Comfort and accept us. Protect and defend us. Keep us away from the Evil One. Keep the Evil One away from us.

Kinfolks is a good idea.

Will Campbell

My Father, I am so grateful that we are "Kinfolks!"

226

For thine is the kingdom, and the power, and the glory, for ever.
Amen.

(MATTHEW 6:13B, KJV)

The conclusion of this divine prayer, commonly called
the doxology, is a solemn thanksgiving, a compendious
acknowledgment of the attributes and works of God.

"For thine is the kingdom"—the sovereign right of all things that
are or ever were created; yea, thy kingdom is an everlasting king-
dom, and thy dominion endureth throughout all ages. "The
power"—the executive power whereby you govern all things in
your everlasting kingdom, whereby you do whatsoever pleases
you, in all places of your dominion. "And the glory"—the praise
due from every creature, for your power, and the mightiness of
your kingdom, and for all your wondrous works which you work
from everlasting, and shall do, world without end, "forever and
ever! Amen!" So be it!

John Wesley

Surely goodness and love will follow me all the days of my life,
and I will dwell in the house of the Lord forever.

(P S A L M   2 3 : 6)

We often quote Psalm 23:6, but I am not sure that we always understand it. Now we don't have much trouble understanding the last part, "I will dwell in the house of the Lord forever." That is eternal! Jesus told us about a house with many mansions and that He is preparing a place there for us.

It is the first part that I am not sure we always see, "Surely goodness and love. . . ." God is goodness and love. He is right there with bundles of goodness and love—with my name on them.

We think that we have to cry out to God, "Where is Your mercy? Where is Your goodness? Why can't I find it?" when all of the time God is right there—every step of the way—with His goodness and love.

Roger Palms

You are right there, Lord, with Your goodness and love.
Thank You.

Your love has given me great joy and encouragement.

(PHILEMON 7A)

When we, members of the body of Christ "get it right," we are an enormous absorber of one another's pain. In reality, the church is a community of suffering. By design we're to share one another's grief and to carry one another's burdens. We are sympathetic by choice, not simply by similarity of experience. We choose to enter into one another's brokenness. We choose to cry with one another. We choose to participate in one another's disappointments and suffering. We choose to identify with one another's losses and grief. When the church operates as a community of suffering, she is incredibly beautiful. There is no organization on the face of the earth like the church!

Steve and Valerie Bell

Heavenly Father, I'm grateful for the love and encouragement You have shown me through Your body, the church.

Rejoice in the Lord always. I will say it again: Rejoice!

(PHILIPPIANS 4:4)

The world uses the word *happiness*, but God talks about *joy*. There's a difference.

Happiness depends on happenings, what goes on *around* you. Joy depends on what goes on *within* you. It is the result of a right relationship with God, a right attitude toward life, and a right faith in the power of Christ. Happiness says, "I am captain of my fate!" and courts disaster. Joy says, "I can do everything through Him who gives me strength" and marches to victory.

Warren Wiersbe

I march to victory with joy in Your strength, Lord.

*Shout with joy to God, all the earth! Sing to the glory
of his name; make his praise glorious!*

(PSALM 66:1-2)

In our overemphasis on "important" things, we often overlook the intrinsic value of life itself. We have begun to believe the radio and TV commercials and have put so many overlays on our life that we can no longer see the fine-grained texture of everyday life.

Have we forgotten how special Wednesdays can be? Have we somehow fallen into the rut where all Mondays are dreary or February is a difficult month? Have we gotten trapped into comparisons and ingratitudes? Are we in the habit of always putting off an experience until we can afford it? Or until the time is right?

"The truth is that life is delicious, horrible, charming, sweet, bitter, and that is everything." (Anatole France)

Now is as good as any time to jump in.

Tim Hansel

*Lord, because of You I celebrate life—every delicious,
horrible, charming, sweet and bitter moment of it.*

When the Lord brought back the captives to Zion, we were like men who dreamed. Our mouths were filled with laughter, our tongues with songs of joy. Then it was said among the nations, "The Lord has done great things for them." The Lord has done great things for us, and we are filled with joy.

(PSALM 126:1-3)

What is joy? Is it happiness? No, happiness is more diffuse, more general than joy. Is it contentment? I don't think so. Contentment is so much tamer than joy. I would offer that joy is the experience of being welcomed, of being accepted, of being celebrated and enjoyed without reservation, without condition. Joy is the experience of being known completely, of being seen for who we are and being judged as good and worthy and pleasing. Joy is the moment in which we come to know ourselves as God truly created us. Joy is the moment in which we come to know another as sister or brother. Joy is the moment in which we come to know God as a God of grace and love.

Peter Jabin

Lord, You have done great things for us, and we are filled with joy!

*Then he opened their minds so they could understand the
Scriptures. He told them, "This is what is written: The Christ
will suffer and rise from the dead on the third day, and
repentance and forgiveness of sins will be preached in his name
to all nations, beginning at Jerusalem. You are witnesses of these
things. I am going to send you what my Father has promised."*

(LUKE 24:45-49A)

I don't know when Jesus will return. I expect it in my
lifetime—but so have believers through the ages. In a
very real sense, when Jesus is to return is none of my
business! What I need to know is what the Lord wants
me to do with my life. I need to know how to make the
decisons that affect next month and next year. I need
to know what He wants me to do today.

That's what the disciples needed, and were given.
Wait a few days. The Spirit will come. You will receive
power. And then, you will be My witnesses—next
door, and throughout the world!

Larry Richards

*Lord, thank You that You don't send us out there
without Your Spirit's power.*

233

*I know what it is to be in need, and I know what it is to
have plenty. I have learned the secret of being content in any
and every situation, whether well fed or hungry, whether
living in plenty or in want.*

(PHILIPPIANS 4:12)

I now began to consider seriously my condition: I am
cast upon a horrible, desolate island, void of all hope of
recovery. But I am alive, and not drowned as all my
ship's company was.

I am divided from mankind, a solitaire . . . but I am
not starved and perishing on a barren place. . . I have
not clothes to cover me. But I am in a hot climate,
where if I had clothes I could hardly wear them. . . I
have no soul to speak to, or relieve me. But God
wonderfully sent the ship in near enough to the shore,
that I have gotten out so many necessary things as will
either supply my wants, or enable me to supply myself
even as long as I live. . . . Upon the whole, here was an
undoubted testimony, that there was scarce any condition in the world so miserable, but there was something negative or something positive to be thankful for
in it.

from *Robinson Crusoe* by Daniel Defoe

*So often we see only the downside, but You lovingly
show us another way to view a situation.*

Now I want you to know, brothers, that what has happened
to me has really served to advance the gospel.

(PHILIPPIANS 1:12)

We find Paul bubbling with *joyous praise* as he proclaims to his Philippian friends the exciting but perhaps unexpected news that his imprisonment is serving to advance the Gospel!

Paul's chains have become a "cable of communication" through which Christ is being preached! Paul is using his chains as an opportunity to share Christ with every prison guard assigned to him as well an anyone else who comes to his quarters. Paul can praise the Lord in the midst of circumstances over which he has no control because he has the assurance that God is in complete control!

Paul's example challenges us to make even the worst circumstances in our lives a stage on which we stand to praise God for his divine faithfulness.

Sandy Petro

I think of what is troubling me most, and use it
as a platform for praise to You, God.

This is the day the Lord has made; let us rejoice and be glad in it.

(PSALM 118:24)

This is the day
the Lord has made.
The Lord?
Today?
Yesterday perhaps
could claim Your craft
or hopefully tomorrow
but not today
this disappointing day so filled
with problems
needs
despair and doubt.
This is the day
the Lord has made
and making it
He'll give me strength
and hope
to take me through.
This is the day
the Lord has made
so I'll be glad
and I'll rejoice in it.

Joseph Bayly

You made it. I thank You for it. I rejoice in it.

God is our refuge and strength, an ever present help in trouble.

(P S A L M *46:1*)

God is forever trying to establish communication; forever aware of the wrong directions we are taking and wishing to warn us; forever offering solutions for the problems that baffle us; forever standing at the door of our loneliness, eager to bring us such comradeship as the most intelligent living mortal could not supply; forever clinging to our indifference in the hope that someday our needs, or at least our tragedies will waken us to respond to his advances. The Real Presence is just that, real and life-transforming.

Albert Edward Day

O God, You keep on patiently trying to get through to us.
Thank You for not giving up.

> *For you did not receive a spirit that makes you a slave*
> *again to fear, but you received the Spirit of sonship.*
> *And by him we cry, "Abba, Father."*

(ROMANS 8:15)

In giving us the name *Abba*, God has given us a personal way to call Him Father, to address Him as a lonely, hurt child addresses his dad. And then He holds us gently in His arms and says to us, "It's OK. Dad is here. You are safe." The words that Jesus used to describe His relationship to the fathering God reveal our relationship with the fathering God. Although He is Elohim and Jehovah in all of the power and glory those names suggest, He is also our Father. The word *Abba* is Aramaic and connotes a deep and abiding relationship. It shows us a fathering God who is approachable and dear to us.

Jack and Jerry Schreur

Abba, You are my loving Father God. You are very dear to me.

*Cast thy burden upon the Lord, and he shall sustain thee;
he shall never suffer the righteous to be moved.*

(PSALM 55:22, KJV)

The Lord does not really lay any great burden on us.
He only wants you to recall Him to mind as often as
possible, to pour out your adoration on Him, to pray
for His grace. Offer Him your sorrows. Return from
time to time to Him, and quietly, purely thank Him for
the benefit He has given you in knowing Him. Thank
Him, too, for the benefit He pours out upon you even
in the midst of your troubles. The Lord asks you to let
Him be the one who consoles you, just as often as you
can find it in you to come to Him.

Brother Lawrence

What little You ask, Lord, and how much You give!

And so we know and rely on the love God has for us.

(1 JOHN 4:16A)

The Lord's love does not fail however much we fail him. Peter had built his whole relationship with Jesus Christ on his assumed capacity to be adequate. That's why he took his denial of the Lord so hard. His strength, loyalty, and faithfulness were his self-generated assets of discipleship. The fallacy in Peter's mind was this: he believed his relationship was dependent on his consistency in producing the qualities he thought had earned him the Lord's approval.

Many of us face the same problem. We project onto the Lord our own measured standard of acceptance. Our whole understanding of him is based in a quid pro quo of bartered love. He will love us if we are good, moral, and diligent. But we have turned the tables; we try to live so that he will love us, rather than living because he has already loved us.

Lloyd Ogilvie

I am grateful, Lord, that Your love for me does not depend on my standards of acceptance.

He has made everything beautiful in its time.

(ECCLESIASTES 3:11A)

One midnight deep in the starlight still
I dreamed that I received this bill—
. . . in account with life:
Five thousand breathless dawns all new;
Five thousand flowers fresh in dew;
Five thousand sunsets wrapped in gold;
One million snowflakes served ice cold;
Five quiet friends; one baby's love;
One white sea with clouds above;
One hundred music-haunted dreams—
    Of moon-drenched roads and hurrying streams,
    Of prophesying winds and trees,
    Of silent stars and drowsing bees,
One June night in a fragrant wood;
One heart that loved and understood!
I wondered when I waked at day
How in God's name, I could pay.

Courtland W. Sayres

So many marvelous gifts . . . freely given, from Your hand.

*In all my prayers for all of you, I always pray with joy
because of your partnership in the gospel from the first day
until now, being confident of this, that he who began a good
work in you will carry it on to completion until the day
of Christ Jesus.*

(PHILIPPIANS 1:4-6)

To encounter affirmation from God, no matter how, where, when, or why it gets through to us, is to experience another piece of wholeness. He does come to each of us personally. He may also show up in the colors of a sunset, or in the silence of a dark quiet room, or in a book, or in the daily push at the office. He constantly hounds us with affirmation. He continually encounters us, moment by moment, with himself. He has come to us; he is with us in Person and in daily personal relationships! He often comes through other persons—sometimes through the most unlikely ones!

Hal Edwards

You come to me in many way, God, quietly changing my life.

In the thirtieth year, in the fourth month on the fifth day,
while I was among the exiles by the Kebar River, the heavens
were opened and I saw visions of God.

(EZEKIEL 1:1)

I looked, and I saw a windstorm coming out of the north—
an immense cloud with flashing lightning and surrounded by
brilliant light. In his vision, Ezekiel was overwhelmed with an invasion of divine presence which he describes in vivid imagery. God came and spoke to Ezekiel out of a storm.

It evokes the image of God speaking to Moses out of the burning bush, to Elijah in the stillness of the desert, to David by the wind whistling through the mulberry trees. God breaks in upon our world, surprising us with His presence and word.

God still speaks to His people amid the storms that blow across their lives. Let us look and listen for God in the storms that break upon us.

Henry Gariepy

I forget to look for You in the storms of life, God.
Thank You that You are there too.

Whatever you do, work at it with all your heart,
as working for the Lord not men.

(COLOSSIANS 3:23)

One of the consequences of human rebellion against
God is that work can become drudgery, and labor can
degenerate into little more than "sweat of the brow"
and blisters. But redemption is designed to roll back
the consequences of the Fall. So what do we do?

First, we head to work thanking God for a new day.
Second, we acknowledge His great gifts of time and
energy and skill and offer them back to Him as an act
of worship. Third, we recognize that work done for
Him has significance and work done well bears testimony to our faith. Fourth, we sense what a privilege it
is to earn a wage in order to support our dependents,
have something to give to those in need, and to offer
gifts to the Lord in worship.

Stuart and Jill Briscoe

Thank You, God, for the privilege, the joy, the fulfillment,
the results of work.

*But as for you, continue in what you have learned
and have become convinced of, because you know those
from whom you learned it, and how from infancy you
have known the holy Scriptures, which are able to make
you wise for salvation through faith in Christ Jesus.*

(2 TIMOTHY 3 : 14 -15)

I am a creature of a day, passing through life as an
arrow through the air. I am a spirit come from God and
returning to God; just hovering over the great gulf, till
a few moments hence, I am no more seen; I drop into
an unchangeable eternity. I want to know one thing—
the way to heaven; how to land safe on that happy
shore. God himself has condescended to teach the
way; for this very end he came from heaven. He hath
written it down in a book. O give me that book! At
any price, give me the book of God! I have it; here is
knowledge enough for me.

John Wesley

*Your book, Lord … what a treasure.
Thank You for what it reveals to me of You.*

Look at the birds of the air; they do not sow or reap
or store away in barns, and yet your heavenly Father feeds them.
Are you not much more valuable than they?

(MATTHEW 6:26)

My little sisters, the birds, much bounden are ye unto God, your Creator, and always in every place ought ye to praise Him, for that He hath given you liberty to fly about everywhere, and hath also given you double and triple raiment; moreover He preserved your seed in the ark of Noah, that your race might not perish out of the world; still more are ye beholden to Him for the element of the air which He hath appointed for you; beyond all this, ye sow not, neither do you reap; and God feedeth you, and giveth you the streams and fountains for your drink; the mountains and the valleys for your refuge and the high trees whereon to make your nests; and because ye know not how to spin or sew, God clotheth you, you and your children; wherefore your Creator loveth you much, seeing that He hath bestowed on you so many benefits; and therefore, my little sisters, beware of the sin of ingratitude, and study always to give praises unto God.

St. Francis of Assisi

Even the birds enjoy your loving care, Father,
and You said we are more valuable than they!

COUNT YOUR BLESSINGS

Let everything that has breath praise the Lord. Praise the Lord.

(PSALM *150:6*)

All things bright and beautiful,
   All creatures, great and small,
All things wise and wonderful,
   The Lord God made them all.

Each little flower that opens,
   Each little bird that sings,
He made their glowing colors,
   He made their tiny wings.

The purple-headed mountain,
   The river running by,
The sunset and the morning,
   That brightens up the sky;

The cold wind in the winter,
   The pleasant summer sun,
The ripe fruits in the garden—
   He made them every one.

He gave us eyes to see them,
   And lips that we might tell
How great is God Almighty,
   Who has made all things well!

Cecil Frances Alexander

*I praise You, Creative Lord, for the world You have made for us,
brimming with beauty.*

Praise be to the Lord forever! Amen and Amen.

(P S A L M 89:52)

"Amen" is one of the great Bible words. It means "so be it." It also affirms that what it relates to is trustworthy and sure.

In the New Testament, it is found accompanying expressions of praise and prayer. But the word has its greatest association and meaning with our Lord. It is one of His most frequently used words—translated "verily" or "I tell you the truth."

It is significant that this word "Amen" is universally the same so that Christians of all nations and languages, when they come together, unitedly praise God as all the people say, "Amen."

Henry Gariepy

May all nations praise You in all languages, Holy God.
And together we will say, "Amen!"

His master replied, "Well done, good and faithful servant!
You have been faithful with a few things; I will put you in charge
of many things. Come and share your master's happiness!"

(MATTHEW 25:21)

Faithfulness has its own peculiar challenges. We live in an environment in which faithfulness is not always highly regarded, where it is even seen as hopelessly out of date. Times change, we are told, and people change. Commitments must be tentative and options kept open. To be faithful can be seen at best as odd; at times it can be downright dangerous, as martyrs down through the ages have shown. But they and we always bear in mind the thought that one day we may hear the biggest accolade of all, from the One who knows—"Well done, good and faithful servant."

Stuart and Jill Briscoe

Lord, You call us to faithfulness in all things. Thank You that
we can look forward to Your words of "well done."

*Then I saw a new heaven and a new earth, for the first heaven
and the first earth had passed away, and there was no longer any
sea. I saw the Holy City, the new Jerusalem, coming down out of
heaven from God, prepared as a bride beautifully dressed for her
husband. And I heard a loud voice from the throne saying,
"Now the dwelling of God is with men, and he will live
with them. They will be his people, and God himself
will be with them and be their God."*

(REVELATION 21:1-3)

The power of God extends to the four corners of the
earth encircling every creature in his embrace. For all
things have been conceived by the Father in union
with the Son and through the Holy Spirit. We feel him
in our bones, in the center of our souls. . . . In time his
work will be finished, the last encircling of his creation
completed. Time will have been perfected. The final
day shall have arrived. And we shall see at last the
perfect power and works of him who was, and is and
ever shall be, who is without beginning and without
end.

Hildegard of Bingen

*What a day that will be, God, when all things
will be new and perfect and complete!*

*I am the good shepherd. The good shepherd lays down his life
for the sheep. The hired hand is not the shepherd who owns the
sheep. So when he sees the wolf coming, he abandons the sheep
and runs away. Then the wolf attacks the flock and scatters it.*

(JOHN 10:11-12)

The shepherd protected from hostile influences. To
keep wild animals at a distance, the shepherd carried a
sling which he learned to use with great skill. When a
sheep, roaming at some distance suddenly fell into
danger, the shepherd could fling a stone with such
accuracy that, landing just beyond the animal, it would
alarm the sheep into turning back for protection. If the
enemy approached too closely, or attacked, the shepherd used his rod. To prevent the sheep from suffering
sunstroke, the shepherd would anoint their heads with
oil.

   Though a hired hand would flee in time of danger, a
genuine shepherd would protect his flock to the
utmost, even laying down his life if necessary.

Leslie B. Flynn

Lord, my Shepherd, thank You that You will protect me.

*Oh, that I might have my request, that God would grant
what I hope for, that God would be willing to crush me,
to let loose his hand and cut me off!*

(J O B 6 : 8 - 9)

Is it any wonder that Job saw in death the only way of escape?

God did not answer Job's plea for death because He had something far better planned for him. God looked beyond Job's depression and bitterness and saw that he still had faith. When I was a young pastor, I heard an experienced saint say, "I have lived long enough to be thankful for unanswered prayer." At the time I was shocked by the statement, but now that I have lived a few more years myself, I know what she was talking about. In the darkness of despair and the prison of pain, we often say things that we later regret; but God understands all about it and lovingly turns a deaf ear to our words but a tender eye to our wounds.

Warren Wiersbe

*I do thank You, Lord—especially as I remember some of the
prayers I've prayed—that You do not answer all of them.*

*Can a mother forget the baby at her breast and have
no compassion on the child she has borne? Though she may
forget, I will not forget you! See, I have engraved you
on the palms of my hands.*

(ISAIAH 49:15-16A)

The greatest gift I have ever received from Jesus Christ
has been the Abba experience. "My dignity as Abba's
child is my most coherent sense of self. When I seek to
fashion a self-image from the adulation of others and
the inner voice whispers, "You've arrived; you're a
player in the Kingdom enterprise," there is no truth in
that self-concept. When I sink into despondency and
the inner voice whispers, "You are no good, a fraud, a
hypocrite, and a dilettante," there is no truth in any
image shaped from that message . . . How would you
respond if I asked you this question: "Do you honestly
believe God *likes* you, not just loves you because theo-
logically God *has* to love you?" If you could answer
with gut-level honesty, "Oh, yes, my Abba is very fond
of me," you would experience a serene compassion for
yourself that approximates the meaning of tenderness.

Brennan Manning

*Abba, my heart fills with thanksgiving
when I realize the extent of Your love for me.*

I have great confidence in you; I take great pride in you. I am greatly encouraged; in all our troubles my joy knows no bounds.

(2   CORINTHIANS   7:4)

When Thielicke said, "We live by God's surprises," he had personally suffered under the Nazis. As a pastor he wrote to young soldiers about to die; he comforted mothers and fathers and children after the bombs killed their loved ones. He preached magnificent sermons week after week as bombs blew apart his church and the lives and dreams of his parishioners.

To Germans disillusioned by the easily manipulated faith of their fathers, he quoted Peter Wust: "The great things happen to those who pray. But we learn to pray best in suffering."

Prayer, suffering, joy, and the surprises of God . . . they are all tightly enmeshed. . . . When we are rightly related to God, life is full of joyful uncertainty and expectancy . . . we do not know what God is going to do next; He packs our lives with surprises all the time.

Harold L. Myra

Oh God, I'm thankful that You keep me guessing with Your surprises, but always reassuring me with Your love.

Once you were not a people, but now you are
the people of God; once you had not received mercy,
but now you have received mercy.

(1 PETER 2:10)

We belong to one family of God and share the same
divine nature. We are living stones in one building,
and priests serving in one temple. We are citizens of
the same heavenly homeland. It is Jesus Christ who is
the source and center of this unity. If we center our
attention and affection on Him, we will walk and work
together; if we focus on ourselves, we will only cause
division.

Unity does not eliminate diversity. Not all children
in a family are alike, nor are all the stones in a building
identical. In fact, it is diversity that gives beauty and
richness to a family or building. The absence of diversity is not *unity*; it is *uniformity*, and uniformity is dull.
It is fine when the choir sings in unison, but I prefer
that they sing in harmony.

Warren Wiersbe

Thank You for the differences in Your family
that make it rich and beautiful.

But godliness with contentment is great gain.

(I TIMOTHY 6:6)

A bishop of the early church, who was a remarkable example of the virtue of contentment, was asked his secret. The venerable old man replied:

It consists in nothing more than making a right use of my eyes. In whatever state I am, I first of all look up to heaven and remember that my principal business here is to get there.

Then I look down upon the earth, and call to mind how small a place I shall occupy in it when I die and am buried. I then look around in the world, and observe what multitudes there are who are in many respects more unhappy than myself. Thus I learn where true happiness is placed, where all our cares must end, and what little reason I have to complain.

David Jeremiah

When I look around me, Lord, I see how little reason I have for complaint and how much reason I have for praise!

*Praise be to the Lord, for he showed his wonderful love to me
when I was in a besieged city.*

(PSALM 31:21)

Last year while fishing at the seashore my line got twisted around the wing of a seagull. He was very agitated so I pulled him gently toward me and let him fasten his beak on my knuckle. This seemed to pacify him, enabling me to unwind the line from his wing with my other hand. He was peaceful so long as he had something to hold on to. We all need someone to hold on to, but that need is not always perceived clearly by the people around us.

Jesus is with us in all of our victories and our defeats. When we are at the very bottom of the well—lonely, hurting and approaching despair—if we will reach out our hand in the dark, Jesus will grasp it with love and strength and assurance. He is there at the bottom of every lonely, dark place loving us, simply waiting for us to reach out in the dark to him.

Leo Holland

*Lord, I reach out for You in a dark place,
and there You are, loving me.*

Show me your ways, O Lord, teach me your paths;
guide me in your truth and teach me, for you are God
my Savior, and my hope is in you all day long.

(PSALM 25:4-5)

In many respects I am very like the swallow. I move through life guided by a force that I cannot explain. By what strange impulse was I impelled to follow this profession—this and no other? By what freak of fate did I marry this wife—this and no other? By what stroke of fortune did I settle in this land—this and no other? Looking back on life, it seems almost like a drift; we seem to have reached this position by the veriest chance. And yet it has all turned out too well to be the result of chance. The fact is that like the swallow we acted instinctively. And that instinct was God! We say with Browning's Paracelsus:

I see my way as birds their trackless way.
I shall arrive! What time, what circuit first,
I ask not: but unless God send His hail,
Or blinding fireballs, sleet or stifling snow,
In some time, His good time, I shall arrive:
He guides me and the bird. In His good time.

F.W. Boreham

I know You are guiding me, just as You promised, Lord.

Your labor in the Lord is not in vain.

(1 CORINTHIANS 15:58)

I meet older Christians who say, particularly when discussing their children, "My life has been in vain. I have failed. I have not accomplished anything."

If we have worked to the best of our ability in faithfulness to the Lord, it doesn't matter what we think of the accomplishment. God will honor our work. The world has its own measure of success, but it is not the same as God's measure. We don't decide whether we have been successful in the Lord based on the world's standards. Our labor is not in vain in the Lord if what we do is done for Him. It will never be empty or meaningless or worthless.

Roger Palms

Dear Lord, thank You that Your measure of success is not the same as the world's. Thank You that anything I accomplish as Your child has meaning and worth.

*I will give thanks to the Lord because of his righteousness
and will sing praise to the name of the Lord Most High.*

(PSALM 7:17)

God's righteousness is without prejudice or partiality.
Other people's responses to my requests are influenced
by their attitudes toward me. But not God's. He
answers my prayers without any unfair prejudice
against me or harmful indulgence toward me. So I can
be secure in His answers.

God's righteousness is His holiness as it affects us.
Since His holiness is the chief subject of rejoicing and
adoration in heaven, when I give thanks unto the Lord
according to His righteousness, I actually am joining
the attitude and activities of those in heaven—rejoicing and adoring Him.

Evelyn Christenson

Righteous God, I join the hosts of heaven today in praise to You.

All you have made will praise you, O Lord;
your saints will extol you.

(P S A L M *145:10*)

The rolling peaks of the Appalachians are so different from the rugged Sierra Nevadas. I walk along a pathway which cuts a swath through high grass and hay bales. On the ridge are silhouetted trees, leafless, waiting for spring.

I see a deer pause in the pathway. I wait and watch her delicate, hesitant movements. When she finally crosses the path, I notice another head pop out near the pathway—her fawn.

I am absolutely alone out here. There isn't another human being for miles, yet I do not feel lonely. Out here there is a greater sense of God's presence. It's almost tangible. Perhaps it is because there is less to distract me. I think my own psalm:

Let all things praise Him. Let the hills praise Him. Let the birds praise Him and the grass praise Him and the deer praise Him. Praise the Lord!

Tim Hansel

My tongue will tell of your righteous acts all day long.

(PSALM 72:24A)

Thank you
for what Deborah
calls minor miracles
Lord
Like finding
a paper bag
a clean one
there on the sidewalk
ten steps after
you prayed for it
or going down
that awful dirt
road
on the side of the mountain
and only passing
four cars
in eight miles.

Joseph Bayly

Lord, those "minor miracles" You work for me every day . . .
today I'll be more aware of them.

> *Devote yourselves to prayer, keeping alert in it*
> *with an attitude of thanksgiving.*

(COLOSSIANS 4:2, NASB)

I shivered in my hotel room in Australia one winter Sunday evening. Chills from a flu-like sore throat left me miserable. Alone in that room, I kept getting sicker and sicker. I took a bite of an apple, but my throat hurt too much to swallow it. And I was scheduled to speak all day, starting early the next morning!

Knowing that no doctor could cure me fast enough for the next day's seminar, I just knelt down by my bed to pray. I didn't ask God to get a replacement speaker ready, I didn't even ask to be healed. I just stayed there, kneeling in prayer with my whole being wrapped in His presence—with feelings of thanks spontaneously flowing to God for the privilege of once again being absolutely dependent upon Him.

I wasn't asking for or expecting what resulted from that prayer, but rising from my knees, I was surprised to find my throat completely healed. Filled with an attitude of gratitude!

Evelyn Christenson

Lord, in Your presence there is joy, and peace . . . and healing.

I pray that out of his glorious riches he may strengthen you
with power through his Spirit in your inner being ... and to
know this love that surpasses knowledge—that you may be
filled to the measure of all the fullness of God.

(EPHESIANS 3:16,19)

One thing you can be sure of is that down the path you
beat with even your most half-cocked and halting
prayer the God you call upon will finally come, and
even if He does not bring you the answer you want, He
will bring you Himself. And maybe at the secret heart
of all our prayers that is what we are really praying for.

Frederick Buechner

O Eternal Christ, understandable to even me, I thank You for
putting the latchstring so low I can reach it. I can reach the
Highest, for You are the Highest become lowly, reachable. And so I
come, for in You I "see"—see everything I need. I thank You.

E. Stanley Jones

*Let Israel rejoice in their Maker; let the people of Zion be glad
in their King. Let them praise his name with dancing and make
music to him with tambourine and harp. For the Lord takes
delight in his people.*

(PSALM 149:2-4A)

In a church I pastored years ago, a young man named
Zack who had virtually no religious background prayed
one morning in Sunday school.

"Hi, God," he prayed, and then he began to laugh—
a simple, honest laugh. "Man, I had a good time last
night. These new friends at my Bible study are great.
Mark and Jeff told the funniest story . . . I'm still laughing. I'm sure glad Bible study is such a fun time.
Thanks, Lord!"

Several other short prayers—much more sedate—
were offered, but Zack's is the only one I still remember. No one had taught him *not* to laugh with God,
and so he did.

David New

It is the heart that is not yet sure of its God that is
afraid to laugh in His presence.

George MacDonald

*Thank You, God, that You welcome us into Your presence,
weeping or laughing.*

How great is the love the Father has lavished on us,
that we should be called children of God!

(1 JOHN 3:1A)

When I was sixteen, I fell in love with Jesus, all starry-eyed to learn that the mighty God of the universe loved little ol' me. A year later, my passion cooled. I'd pick a fight with God and stomp away in anger if I didn't get my way. In my youthful immaturity, my love for God ebbed and flowed like the tide. But His love for me was as constant as the pounding sea. Now, twenty years later, I am confident of God's love. I trust Him. He's never let me down. He will never leave me. And He will always love me . . . even when my emotions deny it.

Lorraine Pintus

Thank You, Father, that Your lavish love is not affected
by my fickle emotions.

But ask the animals, and they will teach you, or the birds of the air, and they will tell you; or speak to the earth, and it will teach you, or let the fish of the sea inform you. Which of all these does not know that the hand of the Lord has done this?

(JOB 12:7-9)

Ask a chipmunk with a body barely six inches long, who made it able to carry and hide more than a bushel of acorns in just three days so he will be prepared for the long winter? . . . Ask the sleek cheetah, the fastest land animal, who made it able to reach speeds of seventy miles an hour? . . . Ask millions of birds, who endowed them with the marvel of migration as their feathered power takes them incredible distances, with the champion migrant, the small arctic tern, making an annual round trip of over 20,000 miles? . . . And ask the brown bat, who enables it to emit sounds at 90,000 vibrations per second and, listening to the echo, to hunt and find its food on the wing.

Let the animals teach us of the marvelous endowments and providence of their Creator.

Henry Gariepy

Your power and presence is all around us, God, in Your amazing creation.

· · COUNT Your BLESSINGS · ·

Now to him who is able to do immeasurably more than all we ask or imagine, according to his power that is at work within us, to him be glory in the church and in Christ Jesus throughout all generations, for ever and ever! Amen.

(EPHESIANS 3:20-21)

God loves to surprise us. It's characteristic of him, like a father who brings home something special for his children. We shout, "Whoopee!" and he adds an affectionate hug. And soon we begin to live with an eye toward heaven. What's next? What's God up to now?

As I've watched God work, I've come to expect the unusual and know that he is in it. As I've paid attention and listened, I've discovered him in the ordinary as well as in the wondrous. I haven't always understood the meaning . . . but the trip has been anything but boring.

Ronald E. Wilson

Thank You for Your surprises. Thank You for the way You do more than we could imagine or expect.

*No eye has seen, no ear has heard, no mind has conceived
what God has prepared for those who love him.*

(1 C O R I N T H I A N S 2 : 9)

Some say, "I can't serve God; I'm hurting. I can't imagine how anything good can come out of the problems I'm facing." Or they say, "My situation is hopeless; I see no value in what is happening." Well, your eye hasn't seen, your ear hasn't heard, and your mind can't even conceive—because your mind can work only with what is—what God has prepared for those who love Him. If you love Him, that promise is for you.

You and I don't have to try to figure out the reasons for all the unexpected things that come along in our lives. All we need to do is to continue to love God and wait to see what God is preparing for us. We know that it is new. We haven't seen it before; we have never even heard of it; our minds can't even conceive it. But God has prepared it and it is for those who love Him.

Roger Palms

*Lord, with thanksgiving I rest in the promise, even though
I can't always imagine what or how you are working and
will continue to work in my life.*

Because you are my help, I sing in the shadow of your wings.
I stay close to you; your right hand upholds me.

(PSALM 63:7-8)

Life is filled with dead ends related to ministry, finances, personal inadequacy, struggles with sin, physical and emotional fatigue—the lists goes on.

When people face dead ends, they want the answers to why and how. No matter what dead end you encounter, you don't have to face it alone; God is right there, waiting for you. It's easy to find Him, once you know He's there.

Ron Mehl

You are here, Lord, close to me. And because You are,
I sing in the shadow of Your protective wings.

*Yet he did not waver through unbelief regarding the promise
of God, but was strengthened in his faith and gave glory to God,
being fully persuaded that God had power to do
what he had promised.*

(ROMANS 4:20-21)

Every promise of Scripture is a writing of God, which
may be pledged before Him with this reasonable
request: "Do as Thou hast said."

Charles H. Spurgeon

The most promising method of prayer is to allow
oneself to be guided by the word of the Scriptures, to
pray on the basis of a word of Scripture. In this way we
shall not become the victims of our own emptiness.

Dietrich Bonhoeffer

*I praise You for Scripture and for the confidence I can have
in the promises I find there.*

For seven days celebrate the Feast to the Lord your God
at the place the Lord will choose. For the Lord your God
will bless you in all your harvest and in all the work
of your hands, and your joy will be complete.

(DEUTERONOMY 16:15)

Inasmuch as the great Father has given us this year an abundant harvest . . . and has made the forests to abound . . . and inasmuch as He has protected us from the ravages of the savages, has spared us from pestilence and disease, has granted us freedom to worship God according to the dictates of our own conscience; now, I, your magistrate, do proclaim that all ye Pilgrims . . . do gather at ye meeting house, on ye hill, between the hours of 9 and 12 in the day time, on Thursday, November ye 29th of the year of our Lord one thousand six hundred and twenty-three, and the third year since ye Pilgrims landed on ye Pilgrim Rock, there to listen to ye pastor, and render thanksgiving to ye Almighty God for all His blessings.

William Bradford
Governor of Plymouth Colony, 1623

Be the meal of beans and pease,
God be thanked for those and these.
Have we flesh or have we fish,
All are fragments from [Your] dish.

Robert Herrick

I will praise God's name in song
and glorify him with thanksgiving.

(PSALM 69:30)

Up with our hearts;
we lift them to the Lord.

O how very meet, and right, and fitting, and due,
in all, and for all,
at all times, places, manners,
in every season, every spot,
everywhere, always, altogether,
to remember Thee, to worship Thee,
to confess to Thee, to praise Thee,
to bless Thee, to hymn Thee,
to give thanks to Thee,
Maker, nourisher, guardian, governor,
preserver, worker, perfector of all,
Lord and Father
King and God,
fountain of life and immortality
treasure of everlasting goods.

Lancelot Andrewes

*Even though I walk through the valley of the shadow of death,
I will fear no evil, for you are with me; your rod and your staff,
they comfort me.*

(P S A L M   2 3 : 4)

One blustery Sunday afternoon in February, I spoke at a service in a convalescent home. Several of the patients were in their nineties, one lady was almost a hundred. She was weeping before the service began; as I leaned over to speak to her, she whispered, "I'm afraid to die."

When I spoke, I asked a question: "If I could promise to take you from this home to a beautiful springlike place where you would be forever free from all your aches and pains, where you could walk and even run, hear and see, and never had any more loneliness or sorrow ever again; but if I had to take you first through a dark tunnel to get you there: how many of you would want to go?" My question was rhetorical, but almost all of those dear old people raised their hands.

"Death is that tunnel," I explained. "It is not to be feared if we trust Jesus, for He will take us through it to heaven."

Joseph Bayly

*Thank You, Jesus, that You will lead me through that dark tunnel
to everlasting light.*

*Early on the first day of the week, while it was still dark,
Mary of Magdala went to the tomb and saw that the stone
had been removed from the entrance. So she came running to
Simon Peter and the other disciple, the one Jesus loved, and
said, "They have taken the Lord out of the tomb, and we
don't know where they have put him!" So Peter
and the other disciple started for the tomb.*

(J O H N 2 0 : 1 - 3)

John saw the linen in which Christ had been wrapped lying on a stone slab, and assumed Jesus' body was still there. Peter stooped and went inside, and discovered that the linen wrappings were empty and hollow! They were shaped like a human body. But there was no body within!

John entered then, and saw the wrappings and the napkin that had been placed over Jesus' face. The evidence was incontrovertible. Jesus had risen from the dead.

There is no more carefully documented event in ancient history than the death and resurrection of Jesus.

Larry Richards

Jesus, the grave could not hold You. You are alive!

The Lord is my shepherd, I shall lack nothing.

(P S A L M 2 3 : 1)

Johovah Ra-ah, the shepherding God, is the Father God who tends to His flock, His children.

This image of God as shepherd always has comforted men and women. The fact that the God of the universe, with all of His power and glory, chooses to picture Himself as an all-seeing and all-caring shepherd tending His flock is almost too wondrous to believe.

The image of God as shepherd also helps us see that no matter what we have done, no matter how badly we feel we have blown it, the shepherding Father welcomes us back into His fold and promises rest in His care for our weary souls.

Jack and Jerry Schreur

*My Shepherd, thank You that You welcome me with rest
and loving care even when I've failed.*

*The sceptre shall not depart from Judah, nor a lawgiver
from between his feet, until Shiloh come; and unto him shall
the gathering of the people be.*

(GENESIS *49:10*, KJV)

Shiloh comes from a verb signifying to *rest*. It is
prophetical of the rest and peace which Jesus gives to
His followers. In this war-haunted world there are
millions to whom this title should give reassurance. He
is able to give an inward peace and equilibrium amidst
the disquietude and turmoil of the outward world.

In Paris, I observed on the Rue de la Paix, a towering
and ornamented monument of Napoleon. It seemed
incongruous that this man of war and bloodshed
should be so prominently positioned over the Street of
Peace. Jesus Christ towers over the centuries of strife
and bloodshed as the only One who can give true rest
and peace.

Henry Gariepy

In You, Jesus, is true rest and true peace.

For the Lord is good and his love endures forever;
his faithfulness continues through all generations.

(Psalm 100:5)

Every person on the face of the earth has personally experienced the goodness of God in many ways. After all, He "causes His sun to rise on the evil and the good, and sends rain on the righteous and the unrighteous."

God provides us with food to eat, heat to keep warm, and water to quench our thirst. He gives us blue sky, green grass, and beautiful mountains. He gives us people to love. Yet so often we take all of those blessings for granted and are not thankful.

John MacArthur, Jr.

For mother-love and father-care,
For brothers strong and sisters fair,
For love at home and here each day,
For guidance lest we go astray,
Father in Heaven, we thank Thee.

For this new morning with its light,
For rest and shelter of the night,
For health and food, for love and friends,
For ev'rything His goodness sends,
Father in Heaven, we thank Thee.

Author Unknown

*God is able to make it up to you by giving you everything
you need and more, so that there will not only be enough for
your own needs, but plenty left over to give joyfully to others.*

(2 CORINTHIANS 9:8, TLB)

God's grace finds us just where we are in life, and that's where we are accepted. If anything was expected before we could receive grace, then it wouldn't be grace! So we don't have to try to be better before we are able to receive God's grace. Even more amazing, though, is that once we do accept God's grace, He gives us power to live beyond our own abilities. It's as though grace takes over and lets us do better. That's how we show grace to people around us—as we are able to do more than we thought we ever could.

John C. Maxwell

*For Your grace, Lord—all that I need
and running over—thank You.*

*Again, I tell you that if two of you on earth agree
about anything you ask for, it will be done for you
by my Father in heaven.*

(MATTHEW 18:19)

You have need not only for secret solitary, but also of
public united prayer. And He gives us a very special
promise for the united prayer of two or three who agree
in what they ask. . . . It is in the union and fellowship
of believers that the Spirit can manifest His full power.

Andrew Murray

*Father, thank You for the special blessing of uniting
in prayer with Christian brothers and sisters.*

As a result, it has become clear throughout the whole palace guard and to everyone else that I am in chains for Christ.

(PHILIPPIANS 1:13)

In her first book, Corrie ten Boom told of her experience in Ravensbruck prison during World War II. As she reflected on her own pain and suffering she came to understand that one of God's purposes was that her suffering should benefit others.

Marine Lieutenant Clebe McClary was permanently disabled when an enemy grenade exploded in his foxhole. His evaluation of his adversity is similar to that of Corrie ten Boom: "I don't think my suffering was in vain. The Lord has used my experiences for good by drawing many lives to Him. It's hard to see any good that came from the war in Vietnam, but I don't believe our effort was wasted. Surely some seed was planted for Christ that cannot be stamped out."

David Jeremiah

Lord, You lighten our suffering when You remind us that You can use it for Your glory.

*Therefore I will boast all the more gladly about my weaknesses,
so that Christ's power may rest on me. That is why, for Christ's
sake, I delight in weaknesses, in insults, in hardships,
in persecutions, in difficulties. For when I am weak,
then I am strong.*

(2 CORINTHIANS 12: 9B-10)

Give God thanks for every weakness, deformity, and imperfection, and accept it as a favour and grace of God, and an instrument to resist pride, and nurse humility; ever remembering, that when God, by giving thee a crooked back, hath also made thy spirit stoop, or less vain, thou art more ready to enter the narrow gate of heaven, than by being straight, and standing upright, and thinking highly. Thus the apostles rejoiced in their infirmities, not moral, but natural and accidental, in their being beaten and whipt like slaves, in their nakedness and poverty.

Jeremy Taylor

*I don't welcome my weaknesses, God, except when I realize
that they give You room for Your strength.*

I have learned to be content whatever the circumstances.

(PHILIPPIANS 4:11B)

Contentment is taking your present situation—whatever obstacle you are facing, whatever limitation you are living with, whatever chronic condition wears you down, whatever has smashed your dreams, whatever factors and circumstances of life tend to push you under—and admitting you don't like it but never saying, "I can't cope with it."

You may feel distress, but you may never feel despair. You may feel pressed down, but you may never feel defeated. Paul says there are unlimited resources, and as soon as you say "I can't cope," you are failing to draw on these resources that Christ has readily, by His loving-kindness, made available to you. Contentment, therefore, is being confident that you measure up to any test you face because Christ has made His strength available within you.

John C. Maxwell

I can walk through this life with confidence and contentment, Christ Jesus, because You are my strength.

I rejoice greatly in the Lord that at last you have renewed
your concern for me. Indeed, you have been concerned,
but you had no opportunity to show it.

(PHILIPPIANS 4:10)

It was common for the Philippians to express their partnership with Paul by means of their gifts, but they had not had an opportunity to do so for quite some time. Paul is thankful for their support, and yet, their concern for him and their obedience to God, fragrantly expressed in their giving, causes him more joy than the gift itself.

God welcomes and delights in the sacrificial offerings given as acts of worship from obedient hearts. To all who joyously display spiritual maturity by generously investing in the kingdom of God, rich dividends are promised.

Sandy Petro

Thank You for the joy of giving.

The Dayspring from on high has visited us.

(LUKE 1:78, NKJV)

My favorite time of day is the dawn. One's soul is filled with reverence to observe the night giving way to the faint traces of light, then those first intimations of the sunrise as the eastern horizon blushes in rosy-tinted hues at such beauty it is presenting. Then there is that glorious moment when the first fires of the sun appear and this colossal fireball rises in unspeakable splendor, infusing the earth with its warmth and beauty and life-giving rays. It's just like God to launch a new day in such extravagant glory!

One of the beautiful titles of our Lord is "Dayspring," which literally means "sunrise." It was very dark when Jesus, our Dayspring, came from on high. But He came as the glorious sunrise, to give light . . . to guide our feet.

Henry Gariepy

Christ, whose glory fills the skies,
  Christ, the true, the only Light,
Sun of Righteousness arise,
  Triumph o'er the shades of night;
Dayspring from on high, be near;
  Daystar, in my heart appear.

Charles Wesley

Praise the Lord, O my soul; all my inmost being,
praise his holy name. Praise the Lord, O my soul,
and forget not all his benefits.

(PSALM 103:1-2)

If life ever seems hard and the future so bleak that you can see nothing but darkness ahead, turn in your Bible to this psalm that celebrates God's love. As you count with David the ways that God loves you, the darkness will break. And, with David, you will be lifted up to sing God's praise.

Larry Richards

Praise You, Lord, as I take time, now, to count
the many ways You have blessed me!

It was he who gave some to be apostles, some to be prophets, some to be evangelists, and some to be pastors and teachers, to prepare God's people for works of service, so that the body of Christ may be built up until we all reach unity in the faith and in the knowledge of the Son of God and become mature, attaining to the whole measure of the fullness of Christ.

(EPHESIANS 4:11-13)

Surveys show that many people are profoundly dissatisfied with their jobs. How can we face every morning with keen anticipation and fresh outlook? Were we to awake to each new dawning with the assurance that the Lord had given us spiritual gifts through which He planned to make us a blessing to others that day, would not this make rising eager and exciting?

If high schoolers, housewives, working men, and businesswomen were to head out each day, not to school or housework or place of business, but to the ministry for which the Holy Spirit had equipped them, would not this help to make the day's employment purposeful, zestful, and abundant?

Leslie B. Flynn

Lord, I head out today, thanking You for the gifts You've given me so I can be Your person wherever I am.

Now we know that if the earthly tent we live in is destroyed,
we have a building from God, an eternal house in heaven,
not built by human hands.

(2 C O R I N T H I A N S 5 : 1)

A high school classmate of mine died this year of
cancer of the esophagus. He was the object of many
prayers for healing in his church before he entered
Johns Hopkins for surgery. I called him before he left.
"Bruce," he told me, "I can't miss. I've had prayers by
God's people for healing, and I believe God can heal.
If he does, I've got it made. If I die, I've got it made.
Either way, I want to serve the Lord and His
Kingdom." My friend Bill had no fear of missing out.
He was focused on God and his Kingdom, sick or well,
in this world or the next.

Bruce Larson

It's true, Lord. Living or dying, we can't miss when we
remember we are Yours in this life and in the next.

Jesus replied, "If anyone loves me, he will obey my teaching. My Father will love him, and we will come to him and make our home with him.

(J O H N 14:23)

The call to prayer is the Father's invitation to visit with Him. This is more than the consciousness of a great need that often drives us to intercession. It is the call of love to come and fellowship.

E.W. Kenyon

I must believe in His infinite love, which really longs to have communion with me every moment and to keep me in the enjoyment of His fellowship.

Andrew Murray

You know, the truth that Christ wants my fellowship, that He loves me, wants me to be with Him and waits for me, has done more to transform my quiet time with God than any other single fact.

Robert Boyd Munger

Thanksgiving floods my soul when I remember that You want my fellowship, that You want to be with me.

But whatever was to my profit I now consider loss for the sake of Christ. What is more, I consider everything a loss compared to the surpassing greatness of knowing Christ Jesus my Lord, for whose sake I have lost all things. I consider them rubbish, that I may gain Christ and be found in him, not having a righteousness of my own that comes from the law, but that which is through faith in Christ—the righteousness that comes from God and is by faith.

(PHILIPPIANS 3 : 7 - 9)

Remember Jim Elliot's words: "He is no fool to give what he cannot keep to gain what he cannot lose." This is what Paul experienced: he lost his religion and his reputation, but he gained far more than he lost. In fact, the gains were so thrilling that Paul considered all other things nothing but garbage in comparison!

No wonder he had joy—his life did not depend on things but on the eternal values found in Christ. Paul had the "spiritual mind" and looked at the things of earth from heaven's point of view. People who live for things are never really happy because they must constantly protect their treasures and worry lest they lose their value. Not so the believer with the spiritual mind; his treasures in Christ can never be stolen and they never lose their value.

Warren Wiersbe

To know You, Jesus, is more wonderful than any earthly gain.

In the same way, the Spirit helps us in our weakness.
We do not know what we ought to pray, but the Spirit himself
intercedes for us with groans that words cannot express. And he
who searches our hearts knows the mind of the Spirit, because the
Spirit intercedes for the saints in accordance with God's will.

(ROMANS 8:26-27)

Lord, I've wept and I've laughed in my prayers. I've told you my
good feelings and my bad feelings. I've screamed out of pain and
danced out of sheer joy. I've been quiet and restful knowing that
you are close by.

You keep drawing us out, teaching us to pray. Your Spirit helps
us express what we cannot verbalize alone.

Thank you for making prayer possible. How could we feel you
otherwise? How could we cope without feeling your breath of life
within and around? I think I'd go bananas!

I praise you for the gift of prayer and for your tremendous
patience with me when I feel so prayerless.

Hal Edwards

For we brought nothing into the world, and we can take
nothing out of it. But if we have food and clothing,
we will be content with that.

(1 TIMOTHY 6:7-8)

These Christians, on the contrary, have a different temper: for each desires only to sit quietly at the feet of the Lord, satisfied with whatever befalls him there. . . . I observed a very puzzling phenomenon here: some had plenty of wealth, silver, gold crowns, and sceptres (for God has even such among His own), others almost nothing save their ill-clad body, emaciated with hunger and thirst. Yet the former professed to have nothing, while the latter to have everything, and were of equally cheerful spirit. Then I understood that he alone is truly wealthy and lacks nothing who knows how to be content with what he has, whether it be much, little, or no money; a large, small or no house; expensive or cheap clothing, or position, office, honor, fame, or none. . . [they] have God for their guardian and ever find in Him a source of living supply of all their needs.

John A. Comenium

Loving God, all my needs, and more, You provide.

He brought me out into a spacious place;
he rescued me because he delighted in me.

(P S A L M *18:19*)

Driving to West Virginia, a friend and I came up behind a van. Some kids in the van put a sign in the back window, "MAKE A FACE." We made the best faces that we possibly could. Then they came back with a sign with big, red letters saying, "THANK YOU."

We decided to join in the fun. In big bold letters, we wrote, "MAKE A PIG FACE." The kids laughed so hard they steamed up the windows. Then they did one of the best impressions of a pig face that I've ever seen.

I am convinced that God loves to laugh. And He wants us to learn how to play as well as pray.

Today don't forget to say thank You to God for His love, His laughter, and His presence.

Tim Hansel

Yes, thank You, God, for love, for the gift of laughter,
for Your presence.

When times are good, be happy; but when times are bad,
consider: God has made the one as well as the other.

(ECCLESIASTES 7:14 A)

God balances our lives by giving us enough blessings to
keep us happy and enough burdens to keep us humble.
If all we had were blessings in our hands, we would fall
right over, so the Lord balances the blessings in our
hands with burdens on our backs. That helps to keep
us steady, and as we yield to Him, He can even turn
the burdens into blessings.

Warren Wiersbe

Thank You for reminding me, God, that those burdens
on my back are balancing me.

And the name of the city from that time on will be:
"THE LORD IS THERE."

(EZEKIEL 48:35B)

The Hebrew phrase *Jehovah-Shammah* (literally, "the Lord is present") ends the prophetic vision of the Book of Ezekiel. That promise has sustained generations of God's people as they put their faith in the Father God, who is there. In a day when fathers desert their children, leaving when things get tough, this kind of God stands out.

Jehovah-Shammah's words to you are simple: "Take heart, I am the Lord your God and I am not going anywhere." The Father who is present always takes our woundedness as His own, understands the fears that drive us to run away physically or emotionally, and bids us stay with Him and learn from Him.

Jack and Jerry Schreur

Heavenly Father, You will never leave me.
You are present—now and always.

Your word is a lamp to my feet and a light for my path.

(PSALM *119:105*)

In Bible times there were no powerful flashlights. The traveler carried a small oil lamp, whose flax wick gave off only a little light. There was enough to see by. Not enough to see what lay ahead down the path, but enough to take the next step without stumbling or falling.

What a reminder for us. The Word of God is a lamp to our path. It doesn't illuminate our future, but it does shine in our present. God's Word gives us the light we need to take our next step in life.

Larry Richards

Thank You for the way Your Word lights up the next step.

Now to the King eternal, immortal, invisible, the only God,
be honor and glory for ever and ever. Amen.

As I read these words, there came into my soul, and was as it were diffused through it, a sense of the glory of the Divine Being; a new sense, quite different from any thing I ever experienced before. Never any words of scripture seemed to me as these words did. I thought within myself, how excellent a being that was, and how happy I should be, if I might enjoy that God, and be wrapt up in heaven, and be as it were swallowed up in him forever!

From about that time, I began to have a new kind of apprehensions and ideas of Christ, and the work of redemption, and the glorious way of salvation by him.

Jonathan Edwards

Holy God, we are Your creatures, and most blessed to call
You the Great Eternal Immortal One, "Father."

Praise the Lord. I will extol the Lord with all my heart
in the council of the upright and in the assembly.

(PSALM 111:1)

A broken ALTAR, Lord, thy servant rears,
Made of a heart, and cemented with tears:
 Whose parts are as thy hand did frame;
 No workman's tool hath touched the same.
  A HEART alone
  Is such a stone,
  As nothing but
  Thy pow'r doth cut.
  Or my hard heart
  Meets in this frame,
  To praise thy name.
 That, if I chance to hold my peace,
 These stones to praise thee may not cease.

George Herbert

Father, I want those you have given me to be with me where I am, and to see my glory, the glory you have given me because you loved me before the creation of the world.

(JOHN 17:24)

Haste thee on from grace to glory,
Armed by faith and winged by prayer;
Heaven's eternal day's before thee,
God's own hand shall guide thee there.
Soon shall close thy earthly mansion;
Swift shall pass thy pilgrim days;
Hope shall change to glad fruition,
Faith to sight and prayer to praise. Amen.

Henry F. Lyte

*One day I will praise You face to face.
Now I praise You in anticipation.*

301

When Moses went up on the mountain, the cloud covered it,
and the glory of the Lord settled on Mount Sinai.
For six days the cloud covered the mountain.

(EXODUS 24:15-16A)

We might be tempted to think, "How fortunate Moses was to see a display of God's glory!" We might actually regret living in this age when God doesn't speak to us directly, wishing that we lived back in those Old Testament times when the mountains shook and the cloud appeared. Or perhaps we nostalgically wish we had been living when Christ was on earth, so that we could have seen Him directly.

We must put an end to such daydreams. The glorious fact is that we are living in an era that has greater opportunities for us than for those who lived in biblical times. True, Moses had special privileges, but the masses of people had to stay away from the mountain. In contrast, today all believers enjoy the privileges which in Moses' day were limited to a few.

Erwin Lutzer

Thank You for the privilege of every day, at all times,
being in Your presence, and without fear.

As the Father has loved me, so have I loved you.
Now remain in my love.

(JOHN 15:9)

"Jesus loves me, this I know . . ." is the most basic, profound truth anyone can ever learn. Jesus loves each of us so much that He died for us. He loves all of us enough that He'll stay by us in our trouble—no matter what! His love remains constant and unconditional. In fact, there's nothing that any of us has ever done or that we could ever do that will cause Him to love us less (or more!) than He does right now. That's a marvelous truth! "Jesus loves me, this I know . . ."

Valerie and Steve Bell

Jesus, You love me, of this I'm sure. Thank You.

Thanks be to God for his indescribable gift!

(2 C O R I N T H I A N S 9 : 15)

Nothing less than Christ's sacrifice would suffice for our salvation. The scarlet payment on the cross alone would satisfy the demands of God's justice for atonement. Had a million suns with their incalculable fires been a sufficient offering, God the Father would have summoned them to illuminate the universe with His altar fire.

Christ as the Pioneer of our salvation made the longest journey of all to rescue us from Satan and sin. He is the cosmic Christ who came through the vast intergalactic reaches of the universe, touching down at Bethlehem, and paid the ultimate price of His journey on Calvary's hill. But by His mighty power He rose again and made His return to heaven. One day He will make His reentry as our reigning Lord to the acclamation of heaven and earth.

Henry Gariepy

What a long way You came, Jesus,
and what an indescribably gift You are.

Or do you show contempt for the riches of his kindness,
tolerance and patience, not realizing that God's kindness
leads you toward repentance?

(ROMANS 2:4)

The act of repentance is actually a gift from God . . . in
the sense that insight into our own broken-world need
and awareness that something has to change is
undoubtedly initiated by God's Spirit. Need and
change are issues we simply would not see or appreciate on our own . . .

This is not a pleasant aspect of God's activity in us,
but it is a necessary one. Similarly, physical pain is not
pleasant when it sends messages concerning our bodily
affairs. But without pain signaling danger or without
God's Spirit convicting when evil is on the loose
within, we would be vulnerable to every hostile
element there is: physical and spiritual. When pain
speaks, we stop doing what we're doing, or we immedi-
ately seek to rectify whatever it is that is causing the
discomfort. When the Spirit of God speaks, we repent:
we renounce what we are doing or thinking and
choose to replace the evil behavior with a godly one.

Gordon MacDonald

Thank You for Your convicting Spirit. Thank You that
You don't abandon me to my own foolishness.

*Therefore confess your sins to each other and pray for
each other so that you may be healed. The prayer of
a righteous man is powerful and effective.*

(JAMES 5:16)

A Christian fellowship lives and exists by the intercession of its members for one another, or it collapses. I can no longer condemn or hate a brother for whom I pray, no matter how much trouble he causes me.

Dietrich Bonhoeffer

The first followers of Christ seem to support all their love, and to maintain all their intercourse and correspondence, by mutual prayers for one another. This was the ancient friendship of Christians, uniting and cementing their hearts.

William Law

*Grateful thanks, Lord, for the fellowship and support
and prayers of other Christians.*

His divine power has given us everything we need for life
and godliness through our knowledge of him who called us
by his own glory and goodness.

(2 PETER 1:3)

Within recent years the ecological crisis in our country
has become obvious. The issue is clear: either we clean
up the atmosphere and live, or continue to pollute it
and die. . . .

The spiritual air we breathe is equally important. We
can live in an atmosphere of complaints, fault-finding,
moodiness, and despair, and eventually destroy our
inner well-being. Or we can live in an atmosphere of
thanksgiving, praise, and an awareness of the workings
of God in the world around us and enhance our spiritual vitality.

Lionel A. Whiston

Father, You are at work in this world, even though we aren't
always aware of Your activity. And we can count on the fact
that You are at work in us.

*I eagerly expect and hope that I will in no way be ashamed,
but will have sufficient courage so that now as always Christ
will be exalted in my body, whether by life or by death.*

(PHILIPPIANS 1:20)

To discover God in the smallest and most ordinary things, as well as in the greatest, is to possess a rare and sublime faith.

Souls who recognize God in the most trivial, the most grievous, and the most mortifying things that happen to them in their lives, honour everything equally with delight and rejoicing and welcome with open arms what others would dread and avoid.

Jean-Pierre de Caussade

*Loving God, I welcome with open arms whatever You
have planned for me, knowing You are interested in every part
of my life.*

But he giveth more grace.

(JAMES 4:6A)

He giveth more grace when the burdens grow greater,
    He sendeth more strength when the labors
        increase;
To added affliction He addeth His mercies,
    To multiplied trials His multiplied peace.

When we have exhausted our store of endurance,
    When our strength has failed ere the day is half
        done,
When we reach the end of our hoarded resources
    Our Father's full giving is only begun.

His love has no limit, His grace has no measure,
    His power no boundary known unto men;
For out of His infinite riches in Jesus
    He giveth and giveth and giveth again.

Annie Johnson Flint

Father, thank You that when I come to the end of my resources,
You are there with more grace.

· COUNT Your BLESSINGS ·

*As Jesus was walking beside the Sea of Galilee, he saw two
brothers, Simon called Peter and his brother Andrew. They were
casting a net into the lake, for they were fishermen.*

(MATTHEW 4:18)

The disciples of our Lord were all chosen from obscure
backgrounds. None of them had any special creden-
tials. But from their common clay of humanity were
fashioned men who turned the world upside down.

And God has been doing the same through the
centuries. St. Francis said that when God called him
He took the meanest and smallest person He could
find. God has done His mighty works through Martin
Luther, an obscure monk; William Booth, an itinerant
evangelist among the outcast of London; Fanny
Crosby, a blind poet who was inspired to write over
6,000 hymns; Corrie ten Boom, a simple Dutch
woman who gave our century one of its most shining
examples of love that sacrifices all for Christ. . . .
Perhaps it is so that the glory may go to the Lord and
not to mere mortals.

Henry Gariepy

*I praise You that You are able to take anyone, anywhere,
and use them to accomplish Your purposes.*

> *Now he who supplies seed to the sower and bread for food*
> *will also supply and increase your store of seed and will enlarge*
> *the harvest of your righteousness. You will be made rich in every*
> *way so that you can be generous on every occasion, and through*
> *us your generosity will result in thanksgiving to God.*
>
> (2 CORINTHIANS 9:10-11)

Get with people and you will get with their problems, but that's also when you will have a successful, productive ministry. Eliminate people from your life, focus only on yourself and, like the farmer with no oxen, your surroundings might be neat and clean but you won't produce anything. So the next time you complain about all the people and their children who keep invading your life, think about the farmer who complains that he has a dirty barn. Do you really want an uncluttered life? Do you really want to have no ministry? Give thanks to God for the people and their children who "clutter up" your life.

Roger Palms

Thank You, God, for the gift of people, "cluttering" our lives.

*For God so loved the world that he gave his one and only
Son, that whoever believes in him shall not perish
but have eternal life.*

(JOHN 3:16)

Megan does not look at strangers the way she looks at
me. She knows I am different. I am her mother, the
one who gave her life. I care for her needs. I love her so
much I would die for her.

Megan's adoring spirit toward me is the same spirit I
want to have toward God. He is my Father, the One
who gave me life. He cares for my needs. He loves me
so much He died for me.

When I look at my Father, I want Him to see in me
a picture of childlike worship. I want Him to wave
around a photograph of me and boast, "Look at My
child! See the grin on her face? the twinkle in her eye?
She gets that adoring expression every time she looks
at Me."

Lorraine Pintus

I adore You, oh Lord who gave me life.

Speak to one another with psalms, hymns and spiritual songs.
Sing and make music in your heart to the Lord.

(EPHESIANS 5:19)

That the singing of spiritual hymns is a goodly thing and pleasing to God, I do not think is hidden from any Christian, since everyone is aware not only of the example of the kings and prophets in the Old Testament, (who praised God with singing and playing, with poetry and all manner of string music), but also of the universality of this custom in Christendom from the beginning, especially psalm singing. Indeed, St. Paul also instituted this in I Corinthians 14:15, and exhorted the Colossians (3:16) to sing spiritual songs and psalms heartily unto the Lord in order that God's Word and Christian teaching might be propagated by this means and practiced in every way. . . . Music is a noble gift of God, next to theology. I would not change my little knowledge of music for a great deal.

Martin Luther

When my whole being responds to melody and rhythm,
I know that music is an awesome gift from You.

*As the deer pants for streams of water, so my soul pants for you,
O God. My soul thirsts for God, for the living God.*

(PSALM 42:1-2A)

I have learnt to love you late, Beauty at once so
ancient and so new! I have learnt to love you late! You
were within me, and I was in the world outside myself.
I searched for you outside myself and, disfigured as I
was, I fell upon the lovely things of your creation. You
were with me, but I was not with you. The beautiful
things of this world kept me far from you and yet, if
they had not been in you, they would have had no
being at all. You called me; your radiance enveloped
me; you put my blindness to flight. You shed your
fragrance about me; I drew breath and now I gasp for
your sweet odour. I tasted you, and now I hunger and
thirst for you. You touched me, and I am inflamed with
love of your peace.

Augustine

*You pursue us, You touch us, and with that touch,
we are never the same.*

All that belongs to the Father is mine.
That is why I said the Spirit will take from what is mine
and make it known to you.

(JOHN 16:15)

I bind unto myself the Name,
The strong Name of the Trinity;
By invocation of the same,
The Three in One, and One in Three.
Of whom all nature hath creation;
Eternal Father, Spirit, Word:
Praise to the Lord of my salvation,
Salvation is of Christ the Lord.

St. Patrick

Praise to You, Father, Son, and Holy Spirit—
Three in One, One in Three.

The virgin will be with child and will give birth
to a son, and they will call him Immanuel—
which means, "God with us."

The miracle and the marvel of *Immanuel*—God with
us—defies description. The hands of God that had
tumbled solar systems into space became the small
chubby hands of an Infant. The feet of God that had
roamed through fiery planets became the infant feet of
a Baby. Jesus was the heart of God wrapped in human
flesh. He was God in the garb of humanity. He was
God walking the earth in sandals.

Henry Gariepy

Thank You, Great Creator God, that You took on
the garb of humanity—my humanity.

The Word became flesh and lived for a while among us.
We have seen his glory, the glory of the one and only Son,
who came from the Father, full of grace and truth.

(JOHN 1:14)

The Greek word for "made His dwelling" carries the idea of pitching a tent.

That's what kind of God we serve—One who camps out with us. One who knows every pebble on our path, One who stretches out on the same cold ground. Jesus left the glories of heaven and poured Himself out upon the earth, becoming not only human, but a poor human, a homeless human, a human who was killed as a criminal.

When we wonder how we're going to pay the rent, He knows what we're going through; He's been there. When we suffer insult and indignity, He knows what we're going through; He's been there. When our bodies are wracked with pain or disease, He knows . . . He knows.

David New

Homeless, insulted, in pain . . . You experienced all of that
and more. For me. Thank You, Lord.

Looking unto Jesus the author and finisher of our faith;
who for the joy that was set before him endured the cross,
despising the shame, and is set down at the right hand
of the throne of God.

(HEBREWS 12:2, KJV)

We used to sing a song in the church in Benton which I like, but which I never really practiced until now. It runs:

Moment by moment I'm kept in His love;
Moment by moment I've life from above;
Looking to Jesus till glory doth shine;
Moment by moment, O Lord, I am Thine.

It is exactly that "moment by moment," every waking moment, surrender, responsiveness, obedience, sensitiveness, pliability, "lost in His love," that I now have the mind-bent to explore with all my might, to respond to Jesus Christ as a violin responds to the bow of the master. . . . Outside the window . . . has been one of the most splendorous sunsets I have ever seen. And these words came singing through my soul, "Looking to Jesus 'till glory doth shine!" Open your soul and entertain the glory of God and after a while that glory will be reflected in the world about you and in the very clouds above your head.

Frank Laubach

Moment by moment, Lord, You hold on to me,
You are present with me.

When I consider your heavens, the work of your fingers,
the moon and the stars, which you have set in place, what is man
that you are mindful of him, the son of man that you
care for him?

(PSALM 8:3-4)

God stretched out the heavens, stippling the night
with impressionistic stars. He set the sun to the rhythm
of the day, the moon to the rhythm of the month, the
seasons to the rhythm of the year. He blew wind
through reedy marshes and beat drums of distant thunder. He formed a likeness of Himself from a lump of
clay and into it breathed life. He crafted a counterpart
to complete the likeness, joining the two halves and
placing them center stage in His creation where there
was a temptation and a fall, a great loss and a great
hiding. God searched for the hiding couple, reaching
to pick them up, dust them off, draw them near.
Though they hardly knew it at the time. After them,
He searched for their children and for their children's
children. And afterward wrote stories of His search.

In doing all this, God gave us art, music, sculpture,
drama, and literature. He gave them as footpaths to
lead us out of our hiding places and as signposts to lead
us along in our search for what was lost.

Ken Gire

You have made life rich with creation—what we see all
around us, and what You draw out from within us.

*I will praise you, O Lord, with all my heart ... Though I walk
in the midst of trouble, you preserve my life; you stretch out your
hand against the anger of my foes, with your right hand you save
me. The Lord will fulfill his purpose for me; your love, O Lord,
endures forever—do not abandon the works of your hands.*

(PSALM 138:7-8)

Live in the now
With all its problems and its agonies
With its joy
And its pain

Celebrate your pain
Your despair
Your anger
It means you're alive
Look closer
Breathe deeper
Stand taller
Stop grieving the past

There is joy and beauty
Today

Clyde Reid

*Yes, there is joy and beauty right here, now, today.
Thank You, Lord.*

*Now faith is being sure of what we hope for
and certain of what we do not see.*

(HEBREWS *11:1*)

It is not only those who are growing old, finding the shadows of life lengthening, who are in search of meaning; there is a desire in every human being to find some kind of unity and coherence, some meaning in the diverse experiences of life. All of us instinctively want to find some kind of key that will unlock the secret and meaning of good days and bad, joy and sorrow, youth and old age, sickness and health, life and death. We want some kind of framework of understanding within which we can find perspective, and be freed from the delusion of confusing that which is truly important with the monumental trivia of life. It is, I think only the overview of faith that can provide for us this insight into life, this meaning of life.

John Powell

Life is confusing and meaningless, God, without the framework of faith. Thank You for showing me what is truly important.

And we pray this in order that you may live a life worthy
of the Lord and may please him in every way: bearing fruit
in every good work, growing in the knowledge of God, being
strengthened with all power according to his glorious might
so that you may have great endurance and patience.

(C O L O S S I A N S *1:10-11*)

This grace of the middle mile the Bible calls "patient continuance." It is a wonderful art that few have mastered. And it gets least attention from the world because there is nothing very dramatic about it. There is something theatric in a big start or a glorious finish. There is nothing for a news reporter along the middle mile. It is a lonesome mile, for the crowd is whoopin' 'er up for the fellow who got through. It's a hard mile, for it's too far to go back and a long way to go on. But if you can keep a song within and a smile without on this dreariest stretch of life, if you can learn to transform it into a paradise of its own, you have mastered the greatest secret of victorious living, the problem of the middle mile.

Vance Havner

Lord, I recognize that "middle mile." Thank You
for the patience and endurance to keep going.

Teach me your way, O Lord, and I will walk in your truth;
give me an undivided heart, that I may fear your name.

(PSALM 86:11)

One of the great privileges of our Christian experience is to have the teachings of Jesus as recorded in the Gospels for our enlightenment and enrichment. Though we cannot step back into the time when Jesus cast His shadow on earth, we can, through the miracle of His Word and the ministry of the Holy Spirit, know and understand those timeless truths He taught during His sojourn here. May we who know Him as our Saviour and Lord also know Him as our Teacher. What incredible truths He has to share with us!

Henry Gariepy

I'm grateful, Jesus, that those who knew You best
took time to record some of what they witnessed.

You are my God, and I will give you thanks;
you are my God, and I will exalt you.

(PSALM *118:28*)

Someone once said, "Success is getting what you want. Happiness is wanting what you get." The Bible expresses the same idea a different way—"Give thanks in all circumstances; for this is the will of God in Christ Jesus for you."

The essence of happiness and peace lies in gratitude. Two things I have learned: (1) gratitude is not optional for a Christian, and (2) gratitude is the source of peace.

If you would really like to change the world within you and thereby around you, learn to be diligent in thanksgiving. Gratitude can be expressed by hard work, by patience, by laughter, by creativity, by persistence, by the quality of your love, by the depth of your hope, and by the certainty of your peace.

Tim Hansel

You are my Lord, You are my life, and I give You thanks!

For although they knew God, they neither glorified him
as God nor gave thanks to Him.

(ROMANS 1:21)

Human beings thrive on encouragement. Even the thickest-skinned person responds to appreciation. A thank you in the right place can travel a great distance. A mother who, having spent hours preparing a meal, watches it disappear in minutes down hungry teenage throats, is greatly blessed by a simple "Thanks, Mom." A harassed secretary, pushed to the limits by a demanding boss, finds new desire to please and new energy to serve once "thanks" is voiced.

One of God's chief complaints against humanity is that, despite His self-revelation, "they neither glorified Him as God, nor gave thanks to Him." This does not mean that God was upset because He wasn't adequately appreciated, but rather, that mankind was functioning in a manner that denied human uniqueness. That uniqueness is seen in the capacity to receive revelation of eternal things, to appreciate them, and to articulate that appreciation in thanksgiving. To fail to be thankful is to fail to be fully human.

Jill and Stuart Briscoe

You have created me for thanksgiving, and when I praise You
I sense Your presence.

Header

*Two are better than one , because they have a good return
for their work.*

(ECCLESIASTES 4:9)

"Loneliness" has been called the most desolate word in the English language. Ours has become a lonely society; old-fashioned neighborliness has given way to urban high rises and private lifestyles.

In one of the beautiful serendipities in Ecclesiastes the author moves from the despair of loneliness to the blessing of companionship. "Two are better than one" he records in his journal. He cites three circumstances: If one falls down, his friend can help him up; if two lie down together, they will keep warm; though one may be overpowered, two can defend themselves.

"A friend may well be reckoned the masterpiece of nature," eulogized Emerson. Coleridge described friendship as a "sheltering tree." A great man was once asked the secret of his achievements. He replied, "I had a friend."

Henry Gariepy

Thank You for the love, encouragement, and support of friends.

I have other sheep that are not of this sheep pen.
I must bring them also. They too will listen to my voice,
and there shall be one flock and one shepherd.

(JOHN 10:16)

Compassion is the sometimes fatal capacity for feeling what it is like to live inside somebody else's skin.

It is the knowledge that there can never really be any peace and joy for me until there is peace and joy finally for you too.

Frederick Buechner

The Savior looks with compassion on his people, the people of God. He could not rest satisfied with the few who had heard his call and followed. He shrank from the idea of forming an exclusive little coterie with his disciples. Unlike the founders of the great religions, he had no desire to withdraw them from the vulgar crowd and initiate them into an esoteric system of religion and ethics. He had come, he had worked and suffered for the sake of all his people.

Dietrich Bonhoeffer

Thank You, Lord, that in Your compassion, You extended
Your call to "other sheep: of whom I am one.

Because God wanted to make the unchanging nature
of his purpose very clear to the heirs of what was promised,
he confirmed it with an oath. God did this so that, by two
unchangeable things in which it is impossible for God to lie,
we who have fled to take hold of the hope offered to us may
be greatly encouraged. We have this hope as an anchor
for the soul, firm and secure.

(HEBREWS 6:17-19A)

True Christian hope is more than "hope so." It is confident assurance of future glory and blessing.

This confident hope does not put us in a rocking chair where we complacently await the return of Jesus Christ. Instead, it puts us in the marketplace, on the battlefield, where we keep on going when the burdens are heavy and the battles are hard. Hope is not a sedative; it is a shot of adrenaline, a blood transfusion. Like an anchor, our hope in Christ stabilizes us in the storms of life. But unlike an anchor, our hope moves us forward; it does not hold us back.

Warren Wiersbe

You are my hope in the midst of the storms of life.
You are my assurance for the future.

For I received from the Lord what I also passed on to you:
The Lord Jesus, on the night he was betrayed, took bread, and
when he had given thanks, he broke it and said, "This is my body,
which is for you; do this in remembrance of me." In the same
way, after supper he took the cup, saying, "This cup is the
new covenant in my blood: do this, whenever you
drink it, in remembrance of me."

(1 CORINTHIANS 11:23-25)

Every time we celebrate the Lord's supper, we are feasting with Him. For the moment, put down your theological wranglings over exactly when and how the bread is the body of Christ—just come and dine. Jesus Christ is present with us, in some way, we all agree. He is the host of this banquet, and He is the honored guest. He has sent His servants out to the "highways and byways" to bring us in as guests, and here we are.

It is a time of remembrance, as we ponder the deep mysteries of Christ's sacrificial death on our behalf. But it is also a time of joy, as we revel in the benefits of that death. He has won our salvation. Let us sing Hallelujah. We dine in thanksgiving for what He has done.

David New

Thank You for the traditional celebrations of the church
that remind us we are family.

And if Christ has not been raised, our preaching is useless
and so is your faith.

(1 CORINTHIANS 15:14)

Paul says the hope of the Resurrection is the reason he is willing to go through intense suffering for Christ. What would be the point he asks, if Christ were not truly alive? By far the biggest problem in life is death. We spend billions of dollars trying to put off the evil day that none of us can escape. But for the Christian the stone has been rolled away from the tomb of death. It's empty! Death for the Christian is the gateway into life. Christ has gone before to tell us there is a new world ahead of us and we can face the grave with utmost confidence in that promise.

Jill Briscoe

Praise God, the grave is empty and You have opened
the gateway to life!

All this is for your benefit, so that the grace that is reaching more and more people may cause thanksgiving to overflow to the glory of God.

(2 CORINTHIANS 4:15)

And suddenly, as I looked at the same cross, he changed to an appearance of joy. The change in his appearance changed mine, and I was as glad and joyful as I could possibly be. And then cheerfully our Lord suggested to my mind: Where is there any instant of your pain or of your grief? And I was very joyful.

Then our Lord put a question to me: Are you well satisfied that I suffered for you? Yes, good Lord, I said; all my thanks to you, good Lord, blessed may you be! If you are satisfied, our Lord said, I am satisfied. It is a joy and a bliss and an endless delight to me that ever I suffered my Passion for you, for if I could suffer more, I would. . . . For Jesus has great joy in all the deeds which he has done for our salvation. . . . We are his bliss, we are his reward, we are his honor, we are his crown.

Julian of Norwich

I am sure that there is in me nothing that could attract the love of One as holy and as just as You are. Yet You have declared Your unchanging love for me in Christ Jesus.

A.W. Tozer

· COUNT YOUR BLESSINGS ·

Those who are wise will shine like the brightness of the heavens,
and those who lead many to righteousness, like the stars
for ever and ever.

(DANIEL 12:3)

E. Stanley Jones is considered by some as one of the wisest men of past generations. Through his insightful and inspiring writings of twenty-eight books, he was a mentor to many of us. A world-renowned evangelist, Christian statesman, and author, several times nominated for the Nobel Peace Prize, he served as a missionary in his beloved India for over fifty years.

Just one month before going to be with his Lord, he wrote, "Now that I am in this crisis I face the question of living on crippled or calling it a day and accepting a passage to the other world . . . I don't know what the future holds, but I know who holds it . . . I have often said half jokingly that when I get to heaven, I will ask for twenty-four hours to see my friends, and then I shall go up to Him and say, 'Haven't you a world somewhere which has fallen people who need an evangelist like me? Please send me there.' For I know no heaven beyond preaching the Gospel to people. That is heaven to me. It has been, is, and ever shall be heaven to me."

Henry Gariepy

Lord, how good You are to have entrusted us with such
a joyful assignment: introducing souls to You.

Trust in him at all times, O people; pour out your hearts to him,
for God is our refuge.

(PSALM 62:8)

O God, immortal, eternal, invisible, I remember with gladness and
thanksgiving all that thou hast been to this world of men:
> *Companion of the brave;*
> *Upholder of the loyal;*
> *Light of the wanderer;*
> *Joy of the pilgrim;*
> *Guide of the pioneer;*
> *Helper of labouring men;*
> *Refuge of the broken-hearted;*
> *Deliverer of the oppressed;*
> *Succour of the tempted;*
> *Strength of the victorious;*
> *Ruler of rulers;*
> *Friend of the poor;*
> *Rescuer of the perishing;*
> *Hope of the dying.*

John Baillie

COUNT YOUR BLESSINGS

But he said to me, "My grace is sufficient for you, for my power is made perfect in weakness." Therefore I will boast all the more gladly about my weaknesses, so that Christ's power may rest on me.

(2 CORINTHIANS 12:9)

On November 29, 1992, Dennis Byrd, a defensive lineman for the New York Jets, collided headfirst with a teammate while trying to make a tackle. Just like that, Dennis' neck was broken and he was paralyzed from the neck down. Doctors said he would probably never walk again. But he did.

In his book *Rise and Walk* Dennis writes: "I could easily have been destroyed by what happened to me. I could easily have just fallen apart. In every material sense I was weak and vulnerable. but there is a verse in 2 Corinthians about that very thing . . . I had become weakness, and I become it in an instant. Only in this weakness was I able to completely lay my entire life at Christ's feet, holding nothing back, putting it all in his hands. He would have to fight the battle for me. And he did."

Jill and Stuart Briscoe

My "weakness" may not be as dramatic, but, just the same, I am grateful that You will be my strength.

Because of my chains, most of the brothers in the Lord
have been encouraged to speak the word of God
more courageously and fearlessly.

(PHILIPPIANS 1:14)

In seventeenth-century England, George Fox and the Quakers were making their mark for the Gospel and hundreds were being converted. In the midst of the revival, while preaching at the Castle of Carlisle in the north of England, George Fox was arrested on charges of blasphemy. After his trial, he was thrown into a filthy dungeon overrun with vermin and criminals. No one was allowed even a glimpse of him. Some who tried to bring him food were clubbed back by the jailers. But 150 miles away, sixteen-year-old James Parnell, a cripple endowed with a brilliant mind, heard about Fox's situation and walked the long miles to the prison. Somehow he managed to get in, and he was never the same again. Says Walter Williams, in his volume on Quaker history, "After he and George Fox spent some time in fellowship together, the lad left Carlisle dungeon with heart aflame, and gave the rest of his life to Christ and the Friends Movement."

David Jeremiah

I praise You, God, for the people You have brought into my life
to point me in Your direction.

Therefore, there is now no condemnation
for those who are in Christ Jesus.

(ROMANS 8:1)

Emotionally, we may live so long under guilt and self-condemnation that the very idea of being free is threatening. We feel comfortable with what we know, and what we know is guilt. We adjust to our feelings of guilt and surrender the peace we could enjoy if we forgave ourselves. If we want to be released from guilt, we must change our thinking. We need a thorough cleansing of our thought processes. No more thinking, "I know what the Bible says about forgiveness, but . . ." Every time we include a "but," we put one more bar in our prison of guilt. We need to get rid of the bars; we need to break out of the prison. We don't have to be there.

John C. Maxwell

Thank You, Jesus! Thank You that You will free us
from our prisons of guilt.

I will praise you, O Lord, with all my heart;
I will tell of all your wonders. I will be glad and rejoice in you;
I will sing praise to your name, O Most High.

(PSALM 9:1,2)

Mary flew across the grass to him.

"Oh, Dickon! Dickon!" she cried out. "How could you get here so early! How could you! The sun has only just got up!"

He got up himself, laughing and glowing, and tousled; his eyes like a bit of the sky. "Eh!" he said. "I was up long before him. How could I have stayed abed! Th' world's all fair begun again this mornin', it has. An' it's workin' an' hummin' an' scratchin' an' pipin' and' nest-buildin' an' breathin' out scents, till you've got to be out on it 'stead o' lyin' on your back. . . ."

They ran from one part of the garden to another and found so many wonders that they were obliged to remind themselves that they must whisper or speak low. . . . There was every joy on earth in the secret garden that morning. . .

Frances Hodgson Burnett

Lord, You gift us with joy when we find pleasure in
Your creation!

I thank my God every time I remember you.

(PHILIPPIANS 1:3)

Lord
I smell fresh bread
just baked
mouth watering warm.
Lord, my mind goes back
mother kneading dough
taking loaf from pan
buttering a slice for me. . .
I smell baby powder
and hold again
a tiny infant now grown
our very own
smelling fresh, clean, human
as baby's mother
lifts him from the bath
Hands baby to me
and says, "Hold him, he's ours
our very own."

Lord thank You
for smells
that trigger memory
warm again with love.

Joseph Bayly

*Remember this: Whoever sows sparingly will also reap sparingly,
and whoever sows generously will also reap generously.*

(2 CORINTHIANS 9:6)

The Christian who is motivated by grace reaps the blessings of personal enrichment in his or her own life and character, and this enrichment benefits others. The final result is glory to God as others give thanks to Him.

God enriches us so that we may give even more bountifully. One of the joys of grace giving is the joy of giving more and more. Everything we have—not just our income—belongs to God, is given to God, and is used by God to accomplish His work. Grace giving means that we really believe that God is the great giver, and we use our material and spiritual resources accordingly. You simply cannot outgive God!

Warren Wiersbe

It is a privilege, God, to give. All that I am and have is Yours.

In the beginning was the Word, and the Word was with God,
and the Word was God.

(JOHN *1:1*)

The Greeks had three words for *word*. One meant the sound of a voice, another was a sound revealing a mental state, and the third, *logos*, combined the thought of expression and wisdom.

As the Word (*logos*), Christ was God become *vocal*. No longer would human prophets give a gradual unfolding of the divine message. God would speak His great and glorious message through His Son. Christ became the ultimate medium of communication from God to man. Through Christ, God speaks to man in a new and living language—the language of life in Christ. Jesus is God's supreme articulation to man.

Henry Gariepy

Because of You, Jesus, I know God.

He is not here; he has risen, just as he said.
Come and see the place where he lay.

(MATTHEW 28:6)

The proclamation of Easter Day is that all is well. And as a Christian, I say this not with the easy optimism of one who has never known a time when all was not well but as one who has faced the Cross in all its obscenity as well as in all its glory, who has known one way or another what it is like to live separated from God. In the end, his will, not ours, is done. Love is the victor. Death is not the end. The end is life. His life and our lives through him, in him. Existence has greater depths of beauty, mystery, and benediction than the wildest visionary has ever dared to dream. Christ our Lord has risen.

Frederick Buechner

O Cross that liftest up my head,
I dare not ask to fly from Thee;
I lay in dust life's glory dead,
And from the ground there blossoms red
Life that shall endless be.

George Matheson

He who loves me will be loved by my Father,
and I too will love him and show myself to him.

(JOHN 14:21B)

In our wonderings, there is one question we never need to ask. Does God care? Do we matter to God? Does he still love his children?

Through the small face of the stable-born baby, he says yes.

Yes, your sins are forgiven.

Yes, your name is written in heaven.

Yes, death has been defeated.

And yes, God has entered your world.

Immanuel. God is with us.

Max Lucado

Yes, You are with us. Praise to You, loving, forgiving Father.

... as the elect of God, holy and beloved ...

(COLOSSIANS 3:12B, KJV)

It is God who has called us by name. The God beside whose beauty the Grand Canyon is only a shadow has called us beloved. The God beside whose power the nuclear bomb is nothing has tender feelings for us. . . . At every moment of our existence God offers us this good news. Sadly, many of us continue to cultivate such an artificial identity that the liberating truth of our belovedness fails to break through. So we become grim, fearful, and legalistic. We hide our pettiness and wallow in guilt. We huff and puff to impress God, scramble for brownie points, thrash about trying to fix ourselves, and live the gospel in such a joyless fashion that it has little appeal to nominal Christians and unbelievers searching for truth. . . Define yourself radically as one beloved by God. This is the true self. Every other identity is illusion.

Brennan Manning

Great God, though I am less than a speck in the universe,
You call me "beloved!"

Then Jesus cried out, "When a man believes in me, he does not believe in me only, but in the one who sent me. When he looks at me, he sees the one who sent me. I have come into the world as a light, so that no one who believes in me should stay in darkness.

(JOHN *12:44-46*)

Jesus, thou joy of loving hearts!
Thou fount of life! Thou light of all!
From the best bliss that earth imparts,
We turn unfilled to thee again.

Thy truth unchanged hath ever stood;
Thou savest those that on thee call;
To them that seek thee, thou art good;
To them that find thee, all-in-all.

Bernard of Clairvaux

God saw all that he had made, and it was very good.

(GENESIS *1:31*)

I thank Thee, God, for lovely transient things,
For luminous clouds and shining, crystal dew,
For quivering shadows and delicate smoke that wings
Its way across a sky ineffably blue.

I thank Thee, God, for vagrant, fragile flowers,
For ethereal forests etched in fairy frost,
For wandering dreams of enchanted ivory towers,
And for faint echoes as of voices lost.

Others may thank Thee, God, for food and raiment,
For guidance along the narrow path of duty,
For power to meet their debts with full, just payment,
But let me thank Thee, God, for fleeting beauty.

Ruth N. Potts

*Thank You for eyes to notice the fleeting moments
of Your creation.*

For you created my inmost being;
you knit me together in my mother's womb.

(P S A L M   *139:13*)

The human eye can see an estimated 8 *million* different colors. It's also estimated that 2 million signals are hitting our nervous system every second. We are Nature's greatest miracle. Our brain is capable of making and storing enough connections and information that the total number would be expressed by a one followed by 6.5 million miles of zeroes—a number that would stretch between the earth and moon and back fourteen times.

We could go on and on. "Fearfully and wonderfully made" begins to take on a whole new meaning. And our attitude of gratitude should be a little more acute, as we begin to realize what special beings we are and what special people we can become.

Tim Hansel

died 1 / 2010

Thank You, God, for the untapped wonders within me
that You created for Your glory.

I am still confident of this:
I will see the goodness of the Lord in the land of the living.

(PSALM 27:13)

During the horrors of the Thirty Years' War, Pastor Martin Rinkart faithfully served the people in Eilenburg, Saxony. He conducted as many as 40 funerals a day, a total of over 4,000 during his ministry. Yet out of this devastating experience, he wrote a "table grace" for his children which today we use as a hymn of thanksgiving:

Now thank we all our God,
With heart and hands and voices,
Who wondrous things hath done,
In whom His world rejoices!

Warren Wiersbe

Only You, Lord, can help us rejoice
in the midst of pain and suffering.

*And we know that in all things God works for the good of those
who love him, who have been called according to his purpose.*

(ROMANS 8:28)

One of the most helpful spiritual exercises to me is
when we who are believers speak God's Word to one
another rather than just expressing our own sense of
sympathy or empathy about another person's problem.
I remember once when a dear personal friend told me
that she sensed God's great pleasure in my courage. At
the time I felt like I was in a great abyss. And in a sense
she gave me a "word-rope" to which I held tightly.

I would say to anyone who is struggling or suffering,
that no matter what your situation is, you can *trust*
God. For me that means, even if my world is spinning
out of control—regardless of how it seems to me—God
has my best interests in mind. . . Somehow He will
work it out and accomplish His purposes.

Pam Wexler

*Even when Our faith and trust is weak, You somehow
accomplish Your purposes regardless of our circumstances!*

Better is a handful with quietness than both hands full together
with toil and grasping for the wind.

(PROVERBS 4:6, NKJV)

We are immersed in a world of clamor, crowds, and cacophony. Sound-soaked days and nights in metropolitan areas bombard tenants with the roar of jets, the din of traffic, the scream of sirens, the tumult of voices. The electronic age intrudes upon us by telephone, television, beepers, and computers. A "handful of quietness" has become an endangered species, and it is easy to miss the accents of the Eternal in the hustle and bustle.

In Proverb's metaphor, it seems that God has given us two hands so that one can be filled with quietness and tranquillity. If both have been filled with the things of the world, perhaps we need to unclasp one of our hands, let go and reach out to take the higher gift God has for us, the gift of peace.

Henry Gariepy

Here, Lord, I've emptied my hand ...
thank You for filling it with Your peace.

We will tell the next generation the praiseworthy deeds of the
Lord, his power, and the wonders he has done.

(PSALM 78:4B)

We are givers of a legacy. The excitement we have, the
stories we tell, the events we recall, and the miracles of
God in our lives should not be lost at our death.

We are an offering; our lives are a gift. First we give
to God, then to others. We plant seeds, knowing that
the plants will come up, because there is a Master
Gardener who is watching and tending the garden.
There will be a harvest and it will be His. We plant in
lives, we give our treasures, we invest words and love;
they all will bring fruit.

Roger Palms

I thank You, Heavenly Father, that the experiences
You allow us can sprout wisdom and encouragement
and love for a younger generation.

I love you, O Lord, my strength.

(PSALM *18:1*)

Little need be said of the highest form of intentional, directed prayer, namely, that of adoration, of thankfulness to God. To pause in prayer and to thank Him for Himself, for His being what He is, to tilt the heart upward to the Lover and be glad, this has a natural place in all silent prayer. An old man was asked how he prayed, and he replied that he just sat for half an hour a day in a mood of profound thankfulness to God. His prayer was that, and that was his prayer.

Douglas V. Steere

Gracious God, I wait before You in silent adoration....

*Then my soul will rejoice in the Lord and delight
in his salvation. My whole being will exclaim,
"Who is like you, O lord?"*

(P S A L M   3 5 : 9 - 1 0 A)

We can thank God even for the sorrow and tragedies
in our life, for even these have a lesson to teach if we
but have the eyes and ears of faith with which to
perceive. . . . To praise God this way takes faith. Such
praise is not always inspired by feelings. It is a decision.
It is a choice. It is an act of the will. In fact, it often
goes against our feelings. But once we enter into praise
and thanksgiving of God by faith, our feelings will
follow. It may take time. Even a long time. But it will
happen.

Praise and thanksgiving of this kind are like priming
a pump. When a pump is dry, you pour water down a
shaft designed to bring water up. You seem to do the
opposite of what is needed. If we thank and praise God
anyway, by faith rather than by feelings, our feelings
will soon follow.

John Michael Talbot

*Thank You for the transforming miracle of thanksgiving
in times of sorrow and trouble.*

He is before all things, and in him all things hold together.

(COLOSSIANS 1:17)

Our globe is tilted on an exact angle of 23 degrees, providing us with four seasons. If it were not so tilted, vapors from the ocean would move north and south and develop into monstrous continents of ice. If the moon didn't retain its exact distance from the earth, ocean tides would inundate the land. If the ocean floors were merely a few feet deeper than they are, the carbon dioxide and oxygen balance of the earth's atmosphere would be completely upset, and no animal or plant life could exist. If the atmosphere's density thinned even a little, many of the meteors that now harmlessly burn up when they hit the atmosphere would constantly bombard the earth's surface.

The universe is a cosmos, not a chaos—an ordered, reliable system instead of an erratic, unpredictable muddle—only because Jesus Christ upholds it all.

John MacArthur

I praise You for holding the world—and me—together.

May the Lord direct your hearts into God's love
and Christ's perseverance.

(2 THESSALONIANS 3 : 5)

Think, Christian, *who is with you*. Right here. Right now. Inside, underneath, overshadowing, *with*. Think how much He loves you, how concerned He is. Think of His cleansing forgiveness. Think of His tender care. Think of His plans for your future.

Stop right now and say, "God loves me."

Emphasize the first word: "God *loves* me."

Emphasize the middle one: "God loves *me*!" Think about it.

Emphasize the last one: "God loves me !"

Ray and Anne Ortlund

Thank You, God. You <u>love</u> me, <u>You</u> love me, You love <u>me</u>!

For I will forgive their wickedness
and will remember their sins no more.

(JEREMIAH 31:34 B)

A priest in the Philippines had a woman in his parish who deeply loved God and claimed she had visions in which she talked with Christ. The priest was skeptical, so to test her, he said to her, "Let me ask you a favor. The next time you have a vision, I want you to ask Christ what terrible sin I committed when I was in seminary." No one know about this sin that was a great burden of guilt to him. He felt he could never be forgiven.

A few days later the priest said, "Well, did Christ visit you in your dreams?"

"Yes, He did," replied the woman.

"And did you ask Him what sin I committed in seminary," he asked rather cynically.

"Yes, I asked Him."

"Well, what did He say?"

"He said, 'I don't remember.'"

Tim Hansel

All praise to You, Christ Jesus, that You have
blotted my sins from Your memory!

"Come now, let us reason together," says the Lord. "Though your sins are like scarlet, they shall be as white as snow; though they are red as crimson, they shall be like wool."

(ISAIAH 1:18)

The royalty of Isaiah's day wore robes dyed deep scarlet and crimson. In one of the most beautiful statements of the Bible, God promises His rebellious children of all ages that, though our sin be deep dyed as scarlet or crimson, He will make our hearts as white as snow or wool. "I will thoroughly purge away your dross and remove your impurities" is the promise of God to the one who repents and returns to Him.

When silver is refined and the dross skimmed off the surface, the refiner could then see himself mirrored in the purified metal. When the Divine Refiner removes the dross of sin from our lives, then our purified lives will reflect the very image of God.

Henry Gariepy

Thank You for this promise, God, that offers hope for us all.

But now, this is what the Lord says—he who created you,
O Jacob, he who formed you, O Israel: "Fear not, for I have
redeemed you; I have called you by name; you are mine."

(ISAIAH 43:1)

Where Christ is, fear is not. One of the saintliest persons I have ever known was a woman in Kentucky who, when I went to India, made a compact with me: she would pray, and I would work, and in the end we would divide the results! When she died, her husband said: "All my life I've been afraid of death, but seeing her going through death so triumphantly has cleansed away all fear of death from me." Jesus has done just that. As you go into the future, remember:

The light of God surrounds you,
The love of God enfolds you,
The presence of God watches over you,
The power of God protects you,
Wherever you are, God is.

E. Stanley Jones

You enfold me in Your love, and banish my fear of death.

But in your hearts set apart Christ as Lord. Always be prepared
to give an answer to everyone who asks you to give the reason
for the hope that you have.

(1 PETER 3:15)

As Christians, we are faced with crises, and we are
tempted to give in to our fears and make the wrong
decisions. But if we "set apart Christ as Lord" in our
hearts, we need never fear men or circumstances. Our
enemies might hurt us, but they can never harm us.
Only we can harm ourselves if we fail to trust God.
Generally speaking, people do not oppose us if we do
good, but even if they do, it is better to suffer for righteousness' sake than to compromise our testimony.

Instead of experiencing fear as we face the enemy,
we can experience blessing, if Jesus Christ is Lord in
our hearts.

Warren Wiersbe

Thank You for the reassurance that I don't have to
face the enemy alone.

I will lie down and sleep in peace, for you alone,
O Lord, make me dwell in safety.

(PSALM 4:8)

The word *happiness* comes from the same root as the word *happening*, suggesting that happiness is based on something happening to us. Happiness is circumstantial. If I pay off my car, I'm happy. If I get a new shirt, I'm happy. If my friends say nice things, I'm happy.

There is nothing wrong with happiness. It's wonderful. The only problem is that it's based on circumstances, and circumstances have a tendency to shift.

Joy, on the other hand, is something which defies circumstances and occurs in spite of difficult situations. Whereas happiness is a feeling, joy is an attitude. A posture. A position. A place. As Paul Sailhamer says, "Joy is that deep settled confidence that God is in control of every area of my life."

Tim Hansel

Lord, You promise Your presence and Your attention to my life,
and I am filled with joy.

I waited patiently for the Lord; he turned to me and heard
my cry. He lifted me out of the slimy pit, out of the mud and
mire; he set my feet on a rock and gave me a firm place to stand.
He put a new song in my mouth, a hymn of praise to our God.

(P S A L M   40:1-3 A)

The moment you reach rock bottom, the moment you
are aware of your utter dispossession of all things, then
you are on the fringe of the kingdom of God, you are
nearly aware that God is love and that He is upholding
you by His love. And at that point you can say two
things simultaneously. You can pray out of your utter
misery, dereliction and poverty, and you can rejoice
that you are so rich with the love of God.

Anthony Bloom

Lord, You are there, ready to put a song in my mouth,
even when I hit rock bottom.

*And the peace of God, which transcends all understanding,
will guard your hearts and your minds in Christ Jesus.*

(PHILIPPIANS 4:7)

Last summer I was sitting in a screened-in porch when a sudden storm hit! The strong winds howled, bending the trees and sending rain crashing against the screens. The lightning cracked loudly in the dark sky, accompanied by great rumbles of thunder. The birds that had been eating peacefully at my feeders screeched warnings as they sought refuge. The openness of the porch gave me little protection as I sat uneasily in the midst of the storm.

As quickly as it came, the storm seemed to end, and I became aware of the overwhelming tranquillity that followed the storm. The calmness and serenity that surrounded me was in awesome contrast to the ferociousness of the storm. Those moments of peace became etched within my mind. God is able to etch a peace within our hearts even greater than that following the storm!

Sandy Petro

*I praise You for Your peace that calms the storms
that rage within us.*

You will go out in joy and be led forth in peace;
the mountains and hills will burst into song before you,
and all the trees of the field will clap their hands.

(ISAIAH 55:12)

I love Thee Lord!
I love Thee for Thy living Word;
I love Thee for the resting night,
And now I love Thee for the morning light.
I love Thee for the early breeze,
The stirring of my poplar trees;
The lapping of the waters on the shore;
I love Thee for ten thousand things and more,
When o'er my hilltop comes Thy glorious sun,
Bringing Thy message that the day's begun.

I love Thee for it all, dear Lord,
For all I see and hear—Thy living word:
My garden laughing to the morning sky,
The flowers praying sweetly—(Why not I?)
Thy summer angels hymning from the hill,
My soul, awake, awake! And be thou still
To hear with spirit ears the living Word—
These morning greetings from thy living Lord!

Ralph S. Cushman

Although I am less than the least of all God's people,
this grace was given me: to preach to the Gentiles
the unsearchable riches of Christ.

(EPHESIANS 3:8-12)

If you were to spend a month feeding on the precious promises of God, you would not be going about with your heads hanging down like bulrushes, complaining how poor you are; but you would lift up your heads with confidence, and proclaim the riches of His grace because you could not help it.

Dwight L. Moody

Oh that I had a thousand voices
To praise my God with thousand tongues!
My heart, which in the Lord rejoices,
Would then proclaim in grateful song
To all, wherever I might be,
What great things God has done for me!

Johann Mentzer

Lord, You lift up our heads and infuse us with joy as we praise
You for the riches of Your indescribable grace.

I will praise you, O Lord, among the nations; I will sing of you among the peoples. For great is your love, higher than the heavens; your faithfulness reaches to the skies.

(PSALM 108: 3-4)

You have made me so rich, oh God, please let me share out Your beauty with open hands. My life has become an uninterrupted dialogue with You, oh God, one great dialogue. Sometimes when I stand in some corner of the [concentration] camp, my feet planted on Your earth, my eyes raised towards Your Heaven, tears sometimes run down my face, tears of deep emotion and gratitude. At night, too, when I lie in my bed and rest in You, oh God, tears of gratitude run down my face, and that is my prayer.

Etty Hillesum

Thank You that when I stop to look, even in my darkest moments there are signs of Your presence.

For you make me glad by your deeds, O Lord; I sing for joy
at the works of your hands.

(PSALM 92: 4-5)

Twenty wild flowers Lord
no twenty-two.
Here they are
all round where I sit
waiting.
I don't know their names
except arbutus. . . .
and daisies.
Maybe I could give names
to the rest. . . .
The rest will be nameless
because here come the children
running through the stream
back from climbing
their stone mountain.

Thank You for wild flowers
Lord
mountains
rushing streams
children
each different.
Thank You.

Joseph Bayly

And I pray that you, being rooted and established in love,
may have power, together with all the saints, to grasp how wide
and long and high and deep is the love of Christ.

(EPHESIANS 3:17B-18)

Today is my birthday. Part of me says, *Today is a day like*
any other day. Don't expect anything special. But another
part of me wants all the people I care about in one big
room shouting, "We love you, Lorraine!"

God wants every day to be my "birth" day. He wants
to greet me each morning with a kiss that says, "Today
is your day. See the sun? I set it on fire for you. Look at
the clouds. I parade them before you. The birds sing,
'Happy Birthday.' All day long, in the heavens and on
earth, listen to Me say, 'I LOVE YOU.'"

Regardless of how you feel at this moment, regardless of what has happened between you and God in the
past, He wants you to know: He loves you.

Lorraine Pintus

Dear God, I love You too.

I will be a Father to you, and you will be my sons and daughters, says the Lord Almighty.

(2 CORINTHIANS 6:18)

Therefore, with angels and with archangels, with the spirits of the just made perfect, with the little children of the kingdom, yea, with the Lord himself, and for all them that know him not, we praise and magnify and laud his name in itself, saying *Our Father*. We do not draw back for that we are unworthy, nor even for that we are hardhearted and care not for the good. For it is his childlikeness that makes him our God and Father. The perfection of his relation to us swallows up all our imperfections, all our defects, all our evils; for our childhood is born of his fatherhood. That [person] is perfect in faith who can come to God . . . without a glow or an aspiration, with the weight of low thoughts, failures, neglects, and wandering forgetfulness, and say to him, "You are my refuge, because you are my home."

George MacDonald

My Father, You are my refuge, because You are my home.

Blessed are the poor in spirit, for theirs is the kingdom of heaven.

(M ATTHEW 5:3)

Those who have found life's true values would not take all the wealth on Wall Street in exchange for the non-material riches that bring abiding joy and peace. Jesus gave the key to true happiness in His Beatitudes. Each begins with, "Blessed are." The Greek word *makarios* translated "blessed" literally means "spiritually prosperous."

No economic condition can deprive us of spiritual prosperity. Such wealth far exceeds the ratings of Dun and Bradstreet. It is not subject to depressions or fluctuations. It is stable and pays fantastic dividends.

Henry Gariepy

My gracious heavenly Father, with gratitude I bow before You today. I rejoice in the little, ordinary things which so often are accepted by me unrecognized and which so frequently pass by unnoticed. For life itself I give You thanks. For the breath which I borrow from You, I am grateful. For the strength to pursue a course of active labor, I offer my gratitude....

C. Ralston Smith

*I will remember my covenant between me and you and
all living creatures of every kind. Never again will the waters
become a flood to destroy all life. Whenever the rainbow appears
in the clouds, I will see it and remember the everlasting
covenant between God and all living creatures
of every kind on the earth.*

(GENESIS 9:15-16)

The text tells us that the rainbow is to serve as a
reminder to God of this specific covenant promise. But
the rainbow means something else to us. Rather than a
reminder of a specific promise, the rainbow is a
reminder of the character of God and the nature of our
relationship with Him. The rainbow reminds us that
God comes to us with promises, not demands; that
God in grace makes commitments to us that do not
depend on our performance. We may fail God, but
God will never fail us.

Larry Richards

*O God, You are totally dependable. Thank You for
reminding me that You will never fail me.*

Ask and it will be given to you; seek and you will find;
knock and the door will be opened to you.
For everyone who asks receives; he who seeks finds;
and to him who knocks, the door will be opened.

(MATTHEW 7:7-8)

My life is one long, daily, hourly record of answered prayer for physical health, for mental overstrain, for guidance given marvelously, for errors and dangers averted, for enmity to the Gospel subdued, for food provided at the exact hour needed, for everything that goes to make up life and my poor service. I can testify with a full and often wonder-stricken awe that I believe God answers prayer. I know God answers prayer!

Mary Slessor

You do answer our prayers, God. One way or another,
You do answer prayer.

Let the peace of Christ rule in your hearts, since as members of one body you were called to peace. And be thankful.

(COLOSSIANS 3:15)

If anyone would tell you the shortest, surest way to all happiness and all perfection, he must tell you to make a rule to yourself to thank and praise God for everything that happens to you. It is certain that whatever seeming calamity happens to you, if you thank and praise God for it, you turn it into a blessing. If you could work miracles, therefore, you could not do more for yourself than by this thankful spirit. It heals and turns all that it touches into happiness.

William Law

How like You, God, to cause something so delightful as praising You to be a benefit to me.

And he directed the people to sit down on the grass.
Taking the five loaves and the two fish and looking up to heaven,
he gave thanks and broke the loaves. Then he gave them to the
disciples, and the disciples gave them to the people.

(MATTHEW 14:19)

Jesus did not seem to need anyone to agree with him in prayer. He and the Father already had an "agreement." The agreement was the Father's will, leaving Jesus remarkably free to lift his heart and voice in thanksgiving and praise: "Thanks, if You can make this food to go around. Thanks, if we all have to go home hungry. Thanks, if You raise Lazarus from the dead. Thanks if we all leave this burial place with our hearts heavy with grief from the loss of our friend and brother. Thanks for Your will. Thanks for Your purpose. Thanks."

Bob Benson

Thank You for Your desire to reveal to me Your will,
and for caring that my life reflects You.

My prayer is not for them alone. I pray also for those who
will believe in me through their message, that all of them may
be one, Father, just as you are in me and I am in you. May they
also be in us so that the world may believe that you have sent me.
I have given them the glory that you gave me, that they may
be one as we are one.

(J O H N   1 7 : 2 0 - 2 2)

Jesus and the Father are bound together by shared
nature, by mutual love, by oneness of purpose, by a
single harmonious will. Jesus lived His life on earth in
union with God the Father, and His actions here
revealed God to us all.

And now, wonder of wonders, Jesus asked that we
may have the kind of relationship with Him that He
has had with the Father! Jesus asked that we might be
bound to Him: given a new nature that is like His, a
capacity to love that reflects His own, a place in God's
plan and purpose, and knowledge of God's will.

What's wonderful is that this prayer has been
answered. We are one with Jesus, our lives are bound
up in His.

Larry Richards

Praise to You, Jesus, that my life is bound together
with You and the Father.

When he saw the crowds, he had compassion on them,
because they were harassed and helpless,
like sheep without a shepherd.

(MATTHEW 9:36)

The English word *compassion* means to experience feelings along with someone. But the Greek word used in Matthew 9 and the Hebrew word used in Psalm 103 are much stronger. Both are based on words for internal organs of the human body. The idea, quite literally, is to "feel in your gut" for someone. We come close when we say, "His heart went out to them."

This is the secret of love: to identify with other people, to put yourself in their shoes, to do unto them as you would want them to do unto you, to love your neighbor as yourself. And this is how God loves us, with a gut-level love that understands our limitations and feels our frustrations.

David New

God, thank You that I am a receiver of
Your awesome love and compassion.

...for I bear your name, O Lord God Almighty.

(JEREMIAH 15:16B)

"At last," he said, as she knelt speechless at his feet, "at last you are here and the 'night of weeping is over and joy comes to you in the morning.'" Then, lifting her up, he continued, "This is the time when you are to receive the fulfillment of the promises. Never am I to call you Much-Afraid again." At that he laughed again and said, "I will write upon her a new name, the name of her God. The Lord God is a sun and shield: the Lord will give grace and glory: no good thing will he withhold from them that walk uprightly" (Psalm 84:11). "This is your new name," he declared. "From henceforth you are Grace and Glory."

Still she could not speak, but stood silent with joy and thanksgiving and awe and wonder.

Hannah Hurnard

You give me a new name, Lord. You tell me that I can shed my name of fear and receive Your name of joy and thanksgiving!

For the Lord loves the just and will not forsake his faithful ones.

(PSALM 37:28A)

The Lord has promised good to me,
His word my hope secures;
He will my shield and portion be
As long as life endures.

Yea, when this flesh and heart shall fail,
And mortal life shall cease,
I shall possess, within the veil,
A life of joy and peace.

John Newton

There are depths of love that I cannot know
Till I cross the narrow sea;
There are heights of joy that I may not reach
Till I rest in peace with Thee.

Fanny J. Crosby

And he carried me away in the Spirit to a mountain
great and high, and showed me the Holy City, Jerusalem,
coming down out of heaven from God.

(REVELATION 21:10)

The Bible describes the new Jerusalem which shall be our home with God.

Think of it—no stumbling around, no confusion, no longer wondering where we are going or what is ahead. No night there, so we won't need a lamp. . . . Why? Because the Lord God shall illumine us, and we shall reign forever and ever. Think of it! . . . Illuminated in every part of our being—lighted and really seeing. That is what it is going to be like.

Roger Palms

When we set out on this quest, we found ourselves moving in the midst of a mighty host, but, as we pressed forward, the marchers, company by company, have fallen out of the race. . . . And now, as we stand and gaze with our eyes upon the farther shore, a single figure rises from the flood and straightway fills the whole horizon. There is the Savior.

Arnold J. Toynbee

Thank You, Loving Father.
We do have something to look forward to.

ACKNOWLEDGMENTS

Reasonable care has been taken to trace ownership of the materials quoted from in this book, and to obtain permission to use copyrighted materials, when necessary.

Abba's Child, Brennan Manning, 1994, NavPress, Colorado Springs, Colorado. All rights reserved.

Celebrate the Temporary, Clyde Reid, 1972, HarperCollins/ Zondervan, New York, New York. All rights reserved.

Growing Strong in the Seasons of Life by Charles R. Swindoll. Copyright © 1983 by Charles R. Swindoll, Inc.. Used by permission of Zondervan Publishing House.

How to Be the Lord's Prayer, Norman Elliot, 1968, Word, Inc., Dallas, Texas. All rights reserved.

Living Beyond Our Fears, Bruce Larson, 1990, Harper San Francisco, San Francisco, California. All rights reserved.

The Presence, Bruce Larson, 1992, Harper San Francisco, San Francisco, California. All rights reserved.

Secret Strength, by Joni Eareckson Tada; Multnomah Publishers, Inc.; copyright 1988, by Joni Eareckson Tada.

Stretching the Soul, Ronald E. Wilson, Fleming H. Revell, a division of Baker Book House Company, © 1995, Grand Rapids, Michigan. All rights reserved.

Windows of the Soul by Ken Gire, Jr.. Copyright © 1996 by Ken Gire, Jr.. Used by permission of Zondervan Publishing House.

SOURCES

Augustine. *Silent Fire*.

Baillie, John. *A Diary of Private Prayer*.

Barclay, William. *Prayers for the Christian Year*.

Bass, Charles D. *Banishing Fear From Your Life*.

Bayly, Joseph. *Heaven*.

Bayly, Joseph. *The Last Thing We Talk About*.

Bayly, Joseph. *Psalms of My Life*.

Bell, Steve. *Back to Your Spiritual Future*.

Bell, Steve and Valerie. *Coming Back*.

Benson, Bob. *He Speaks Softly*.

Bloom, Anthony. *Beginning to Pray*.

Bonhoeffer, Dietrich. *The Cost of Discipleship*.

Briscoe, Jill. *The Heartbeat of Jesus*.

Briscoe, Stuart and Jill. *Family Book of Christian Values*.

Buechner, Frederick. *Now and Then*.

Buechner, Frederick. *Wishful Thinking*.

Bunyan, John. *The Spiritual Riches of John Bunyan*.

Campbell, Will. *God on Earth*.

Chambers, Oswald. *My Utmost for His Highest*.

Christenson, Evelyn. *What Happens When God Answers Prayer*.

Crosby, Fanny J. *To God Be the Glory*.

Cushman, Ralph S. *Practicing the Presence*.

Day, Albert Edward. *The Capitvating Presence*.

de Caussade, Jean-Pierre. *Sacrament of the Present Moment*.

Doherty, Catherine de Hueck. *Poustinia: Christian Spirituality of East*.

Edwards, Hal. *The Gift of Wholeness*.

Elliott, Norman. *How to Be the Lord's Prayer*.

Farrell, Edward. *Surprised by the Spirit*.

Ferguson, David, Teresa, Terri. Warren, Paul and Vicky. *Intimate Family Moments*.

Finney, Charles. Shoemaker, Samuel M. *Prayer Power Points* (compiled by Randall Roth).

Flint, Annie Johnson. *He Giveth More Grace*.

Flynn, Leslie B. *19 Gifts of the Spirit*.

Fosdick, Harry Emerson. *The Meaning of Prayer*.

Foster, Richard J. *The Celebration of Discipline*.

Gariepy, Henry. *100 Portraits of Christ.*
Gariepy, Henry. *Light in a Dark Place.*
Gariepy, Henry. *Wisdom to Live By.*
Gire, Ken. *Windows of the Soul.*
Hallesby, O. *Prayer.*
Hansel, Tim. *Keep On Dancin'.*
Havner, Vance. *Consider Him.*
Hildegard of Bingen. *Let There Be Light.*
Hillesum, Etty. *An Interrupted Life.*
Holland, Leo. *Images of God.*
Hurnard, Hannah. *Hinds Feet on High Places.*
Jeffress, Robert. *Choose Your Attitude, Change Your Life.*
Jeremiah, David. *Turning Toward Joy.*
Jones, E. Stanley. *The Way.*
Julian of Norwich. *Showings.*
Kelsey, Morton T. *The Other Side of Silence.*
Klug, Ron. *Growing in Joy.*
Labat, Elizabeth-Paule. *The Presence of God.*
Larson, Bruce. *Living Beyond Our Fears.*
Larson, Bruce. *The Presence.*
Lucado, Max. *He Still Moves Stones.*
Lutzer, Erwin. *Getting Closer to God.*
MacArthur Jr., John. *First Love.*
MacDonald, George. *An Anthology of George MacDonald.*
MacDonald, George. *Creation in Christ.*
MacDonald, Gordon. *Rebuilding Your Broken World.*
Mains, David. *Never Too Late to Dream.*
Manning, Brennan. *Abba's Child.*
Marshall, Catherine. *Something More.*
Maxwell, John C. *Be a People Person.*
Maxwell, John C. *Your Family Time With God.*
Mehl, Ron. *Charisma*, Nov. '96.
Merton, Thomas. *Thoughts in Solitude.*
Meyer, F.B. *Devotional Commentary on Philippians.*
Morley, Patrick M. *Walking with Christ in the Details of Life.*
Muggeridge, Malcolm. *Something Beautiful for God.*
Murray, Andrew. *With Christ in the School of Prayer.*
New, David. *How to Fear God.*
Nouwen, Henri J. *Gracias!*
Nouwen, Henri J.M. *The Genesee Diary.*
O'Connor, Elizabeth. *The Eighth Day.*
Ogilvie, Lloyd. *Ask Him Anything.*
Ortlund, Ray and Anne. *In His Presence.*
Owens, Virginia Stem. *And the Trees Clap Their Hands.*

Palms, Roger. *Celebrate Life After 50.*

Pennington, M. Basil. *A Place Apart.*

Peterson, Eugene H. *A Long Odedience in the Same Direction.*

Petro, Sandy. *Spice Up Your Life With Joy.*

Pettepiece, Thomas G. *Visions of a World Hungry.*

Pinnock, Clark H., Brow, Robert C. *Unbounded Love.*

Pintus, Lorraine. *Diapers, Pacifiers and Other Holy Things.*

Pippert, Rebecca Manley. *Out of the Saltshaker.*

Powell, John. *A Reason to Live, A Reason to Die.*

Reid, Clyde. *Celebrate the Temporary.*

Rice, Helen Steiner. *Daily Stepping Stones.*

Richards, Larry. *Devotional Commentary.*

Sayres, Courtland W. *Wisdom to Live By.*

Schreur, Jack and Jerry. *Fathers and Daughters.*

Schreur, Jack and Jerry. *Fathers and Sons.*

Scupoli, Lorenzo. *Great Is Thy Faithfulness.*

Shlemon, Barbara. *Living Each Day by the Power of Faith.*

Shoemaker, Samuel M. *With the Holy Spirit and With Fire.*

Smith, Hannah Whitall. *The Christian's Secret of a Happy Life.*

Stanley, Charles F. *The Heart of Praise.*

Stewart, James S. *Heralds of God.*

Swindoll, Charles R. *Growing Strong in the Seasons of Life.*

Tada, Joni Eareckson. *Secret Strength.*

Talbot, John Michael. *Blessings, Reflections on Beatitudes.*

Taylor, J. Hudson. *To China With Love.*

Thielicke, Helmut. *In Death and Life.*

Thomas, Gary. *Moody Monthly*, Nov./Dec. '96.

Thurman, Howard. *The Growing Edge.*

Thurman, Howard. *The Inward Journey.*

Tozer, A.W. *The Pursuit of God.*

Wangerin Jr., Walter. *Ragman and Other Cries of Faith.*

Wesley, John. *Christian Perfection.*

Wesley, John. *The John Wesley Reader.*

Whiston, Lionel A. *Enjoy the Journey.*

Wiersbe, Warren. *Comfort: A 30 Day Devotional.*

Wiersbe, Warren. *Contentment: A 30 Day Devotional.*

Wiersbe, Warren. *Encouragement: A 30 Day Devotional.*

Wiersbe, Warren. *Hope: A 30 Day Devotional.*

Wiersbe, Warren. *Joy: A 30 Day Devotional.*

Wiersbe, Warren. *Patience: A 30 Day Devotional.*

Wiersbe, Warren. *Renewal: A 30 Day Devotional.*

Wilson, Ronald E. *Stretching the Soul.*

Yancey, Philip. *Disappointment with God.*

INDEX

Bible 13, 18, 29, 56, 73, 143, 164, 194, 220, 227, 273, 293, 323

Creation 32, 45, 75, 114, 165, 215, 243, 249, 263, 269, 319, 337, 345, 347, 362, 365

Eternal Life/Heaven 17, 21, 28, 51, 77, 121, 123, 147, 156, 173, 189, 198, 218, 223, 228, 250, 276, 290, 301, 330, 377, 378

Family/Friends 38, 81, 100, 116, 126, 127, 152, 157, 187, 203, 257, 311, 326, 338

Fellowship of Believers 26, 31, 34, 37, 55, 60, 81, 100, 109, 116, 126, 127, 178, 210, 229, 250, 257, 282, 286, 306, 335

Forgiveness 46, 51, 68, 69, 75, 101, 148, 151, 176, 177, 305, 336, 353, 356

Gifts 34, 100, 109, 186, 192, 289, 310

God 59, 61, 70, 72, 82, 87, 110, 124, 150, 154, 163, 174, 206, 215, 227, 270, 299, 314, 315, 369

God's Love and Care 16, 22, 27, 47, 70, 71, 79, 80, 85, 92, 108, 110, 111, 112, 136, 137, 138, 144, 150, 155, 161, 162, 168, 177, 187, 190, 191, 199, 200, 201, 213, 223, 225, 226, 228, 237, 239, 240, 242, 248, 255, 256, 259, 268, 271, 278, 281, 294, 303, 308, 312, 313, 331, 342, 343, 348, 354, 360, 367, 368, 375, 376

God's Presence 24, 35, 40, 57, 58, 72, 83, 84, 85, 98, 128, 142, 174, 188, 200, 204, 211, 214, 228, 239, 244, 245, 266, 272, 291, 297, 302, 318, 354, 357, 358

Grace 76, 96, 106, 113, 124, 148, 153, 154, 155, 179, 201, 281, 309, 363

Grateful Heart/Praise 11, 12, 19, 22, 28, 33, 42, 43, 52, 53, 66, 67, 80, 82, 83, 92, 93, 102, 103, 105, 106, 118, 119, 120, 131, 132, 133, 145, 146, 159, 160, 163, 166, 170, 171, 172, 183, 184, 191, 194, 195, 196, 207, 209, 211, 227, 235, 236, 241, 248, 250, 254, 258, 262, 263, 264, 265, 274, 275, 280, 288, 295, 299, 300, 307, 320, 321, 324, 325, 333, 337, 338, 347, 351, 352, 360, 363, 364, 369, 372

Guidance 16, 30, 54, 72, 76, 86, 87, 88, 89, 101, 142, 163, 205, 212, 233, 237, 256, 260, 348

Healing/Restoration/Growth 84, 85, 101, 151, 154, 155, 161, 167, 177, 184, 189, 202, 238, 265, 306

Holy Spirit 14, 20, 31, 41, 63, 120, 138, 233, 293, 305, 315

Hope 30, 46, 58, 62, 77, 84, 117, 121, 134, 147, 158, 183, 207, 219, 224, 260, 271, 290, 328, 350, 377

Jesus 15, 27, 35, 37, 49, 57, 65, 68, 69, 70, 88, 95, 97, 98, 122, 128, 129, 130, 131, 134, 164, 170, 175, 176, 181, 199, 216, 221, 222, 253, 277, 287, 303, 304, 315, 316, 317, 318, 327, 329, 330, 331, 340, 341, 343, 353, 358, 373, 374

Joy 30, 36, 44, 50, 60, 76, 78, 90, 91, 136, 137, 162, 168, 180, 185, 219, 230, 231, 232, 235, 236, 256, 286, 293, 295, 313, 320, 322, 339, 359, 376

Material/Physical Needs 23, 80, 89, 94, 105, 203, 212, 234, 237, 248, 274, 281, 294

Peace/Rest 24, 36, 39, 74, 85, 140, 141, 162, 181, 205, 234, 279, 285, 349, 361

Prayer 14, 39, 47, 55, 64, 99, 123, 131, 145, 160, 161, 178, 182, 212, 238, 254, 265, 266, 267, 282, 291, 293, 306, 371

Salvation 48, 51, 52, 68, 69, 75, 98, 104, 177, 194, 276, 292, 304, 329, 336, 341

Service 19, 25, 26, 41, 48, 49, 59, 60, 65, 86, 90, 91, 93, 104, 110, 113, 115, 117, 125, 130, 135, 144, 186, 192, 233, 246, 251, 261, 283, 310, 311, 322, 332, 339, 350

Strength/Comfort/Courage 17, 54, 62, 63, 86, 93, 96, 97, 103, 117, 135, 193, 202, 208, 210, 217, 241, 259, 270, 283, 284, 285, 322, 334